SOCIAL ANXIETY:

*A Complete Effective Guide for
Overcoming Anxiety, Panic Attacks,
and
Social Phobia Through Mindfulness*

*By
Alex C. Wolf*

Table of Contents

Introduction

Congratulations on purchasing *Social Anxiety* and thank you for doing so.

The following chapters will discuss how to overcome anxiety, panic attacks, and social phobia through mindfulness meditation and cognitive behavioral therapy. Anxiety disorder is a common but debilitating mental illness, and this book shows you methods and exercises to overcome it.

We'll take an in-depth look at generalized anxiety, social phobias, and panic attacks, along with providing ways to identify them and treat them yourself. Cognitive behavioral therapy, or CBT, is a therapy you can work through yourself, and some of the chapters in this book are dedicated to teaching you how to do just that. Mindfulness is another great tool against anxiety, and we'll guide you through it.

Social Anxiety not only explains anxiety in detail and describes different methods for dealing with it, it also gives you tips and tools to keep yourself going strong. This book is designed to be a guide all the way through your anxiety and on to the other side. You can refer back to it whenever you need a refresher on anything involving your anxiety disorder. You'll also find journal exercises, quotes, and inspirations to light up your journey.

There are plenty of books on this subject on the market, so thanks again for choosing this one! Every effort was made to ensure it is full of as much useful information as possible, so please enjoy!

Chapter 1: Living with Anxiety

"Worry is my worst enemy...an enemy I unleash upon myself." – Terri Guillemets

Everyone experiences anxiety at some point in their lives. It's a common reaction to stressful situations. In most cases, it can be a useful tool. Reflexes are quickened, attention is hyper-focused, heart rate increases, and the body is prepared to act immediately. Normal anxiety responds to an immediate threat, and fades once the threat has passed. However, for those of us with an anxiety disorder, this happens more frequently and more intensely than it should.

Back in the so-called caveman days, anxiety was particularly useful. It put the body and brain into "fight or flight" mode, directing the body's resources from cognitive activity to the muscles and heart. This was key to escaping or avoiding a deadly threat. Unfortunately for a lot of us, the brain responds in a similar way to things it perceives dangerous today. We're rarely being chased by a saber-toothed tiger though; our dangers are more perceived threats, more abstract ideas that may not physically hurt us, but could damage us mentally.

The brain is a fascinating organ that can do complex calculations in a matter of milliseconds. As soon as it receives some sort of stimuli, it decides whether or not it's a threat. If it is, the small section called the amygdala is activated before the thought is even registered. This is what turns down cognitive function while boosting physical functions for a fight or flight situation.

If the brain doesn't see a threat, it will send the information to the hippocampus to be processed as a thought. Because of all the work the brain has to do, it likes to find shortcuts. These shortcuts are often the root of excess anxiety. It's a complicated thing that we'll discuss in further chapters, but the brain gets around processing a danger by looking for previous information on a similar situation. With anxiety disorders, the past experiences or thoughts incorrectly inform the present scenario.

You might think some of the reactions above sound familiar, but let's talk about what they look like in an everyday situation. Mentally, anxiety brings on racing thoughts, a sense of fear or dread, worries that seem impossible to control, panic, feelings of losing control, a sense of imminent doom, irritability, and sometimes a sense of detachment from oneself.

Physically, you might experience shortness of breath, faster heart rate, sweating, chills or hot flashes, sweating, trembling or shaking, nausea or other stomach unrest, knots in the stomach or chest, dizziness or light-headedness, numbness, a feeling of choking, and chest pain. Any or all of these things may be felt when anxiety is high, and hits with intensity during panic attacks.

Anxiety disorders trigger these symptoms at perceived threats brought on by false beliefs or assumptions. It happens more frequently, with more intensity, and for longer periods of time than it would for someone not suffering from this disorder. The anxiety feels uncontrollable, and the sufferer often has a sense they are spiraling out of control. This leads to more anxiety and creates a vicious cycle. The more the symptoms occur, the harder it is to break the circle. This makes it a particularly tricky mental illness to treat, and it takes a lot of willpower.

The physical symptoms of anxiety bring on further health issues in the body. When the amygdala senses a threat, it activates the adrenal glands and the body is flooded with cortisol. This is the stress hormone that controls the fight-or-flight instinct. That isn't the only thing it does, though. It also controls how your body processes proteins, fats, and carbohydrates, manages inflammation, regulates blood pressure, raises blood sugar when necessary, dictates your sleep/wake cycle, and can provide energy boosts.

When cortisol levels are off, all of these things suffer. When it's frequently out of balance, like it is with an anxiety disorder, it can lead to problems such as headaches or migraines, heart disease, difficulty concentrating, memory problems, digestive issues, insomnia, and weight gain, in addition to further anxiety and depression.

Because of this, anxiety sufferers are often below ideal physical health levels. This can create a chain reaction to even more health problems. Frequent illness leads to even more stress, as well as the things that come along with it, such as medical visits, procedures, and the bills that come along with them.

ALEX C. WOLF

Along with the internal struggles, anxiety can come with social issues as well. Unfortunately, in some places there is still stigma against mental health disorders. If you live in such an area or know people who hold these beliefs, you may keep silent about your own problems or suffer whenever you do speak about them. Either way, it further wears on you.

Even if you are surrounded by tolerant people, anxiety is difficult to understand for people who have never experienced it. Even caring and kind people may think that you need to "just stop worrying" or "cheer up" to be better. It can be exhausting to deal with, but keep in mind that an anxiety disorder is very difficult for someone to imagine having. Mental illness has unpredictable effects on the mind, and people who haven't experienced it won't understand it much.

Anxiety is sometimes difficult to talk about, and to find good information about. There are quite a few myths surrounding it due to stigma and ignorance. Even sufferers may believe some of the myths, simply because they've heard them so much. One is that anyone with anxiety needs to avoid stress and hard situations. However, trying to avoid your anxiety actually aggravates it.

Don't treat yourself as fragile, because you aren't. You can do anything you want or need to, and it won't damage your psyche. If you find someone treating you with kid gloves, feel free to speak up and kindly tell them some facts about your anxiety. You might even give them some suggestions on how they can actually help someone with mental disorders.

Some people may not realize how severe an anxiety disorder is. This can be because everyone feels some anxiety at some point. For people who don't have a disorder, it's a brief emotion that has minimal impact and goes away as soon as they're out of a stressful situation. This leads to some people believing it's the same thing with an anxiety disorder. However, with a disorder, the feelings are much more intense, don't always have a reason for showing up, and last a lot longer.

If you suffer from anxiety, a lot of this probably sounds familiar to you. You might even be realizing that your anxiety affects more than you thought, and that some other problems in your life could be attributed to it. Take some time to consider the various areas of your life you would like to improve. Do you think your anxiety might be playing a role in any of them?

It's recommended to start a journal, as it can play a key part of recovery. If you have one, write down the ways your anxiety affects your life. This is a great first step to overcoming it – once you see how much stems from that single issue, an issue you can handle, you'll have a bit more hope.

Getting treatment for your anxiety is important, but a lot of people who suffer from it don't. They may not believe they actually have a problem that needs to be treated. Some of them have personal beliefs against seeking help for emotional problems. It's possible you might not yet realize how bad your disorder is, or think it's not worth seeking treatment for.

There are even cases where people think others have it so much worse, so their case isn't worthy of taking up someone's attention. However, everyone who is suffering deserves help. Going without treatment will only make the condition worse. It's impossible to live a happy, healthy life while ignoring chronic anxiety.

How do you know when it's time to seek treatment? If it's preventing you from engaging in normal functions, like social, academic, work, or pleasant activities, or you can participate in these things but with a huge amount of discomfort, it's time to look into ways to lessen the anxiety. Anxiety may prevent someone from driving, or visiting certain places. They might avoid situations that involve public speaking, or any confrontation. Anything like this has a profound impact on your life.

Another sign your anxiety is controlling your life is certain "safety behaviors." These are coping methods you've developed to protect yourself. Avoiding eye contact while speaking, taking the long route instead of driving on an interstate, only speaking to people you already know at events, or obsessively checking that you have your cell phone in case of an emergency are some examples of this. These behaviors make you feel safer and help you to avoid sources of anxiety, but they also affect how you function.

If panic attacks are common for you, you might reach the point where you're afraid to go to certain places or even leave your house. Anxiety attacks are terrifying, and legitimately make you afraid that you're dying. The first few are the scariest, since you may not know what's happening.

If you don't have a healthy way to shut down panic attacks, you might just avoid the situations that seemed to cause them in the first place. You don't want to deal with the physical symptoms, mental distress, or possible embarrassment of someone witnessing you go through this. Instead of finding ways to make it stop, you might choose to not leave your home.

People with untreated anxiety will rarely stand up for themselves or ask for what they want. They place other's comfort and needs above their own so they don't have to protest against them. Confrontation is avoided at all costs. You might lend your expensive cordless drill to your neighbor, and never ask for it back.

He may have accidentally set it aside and forgot about it, and will return it as soon as you ask, but you can't stand the thought of a possible unpleasant interaction. Situations like this happen for anxious people all the time. Because of this, they are constantly taken advantage of, inadvertently or not. They rarely do what they want or engage in things that will make them happy.

Constant worrying is one of the classic signs of anxiety, and letting it go unchecked makes your whole life miserable. People who do not have a mental disorder have the ability to turn their worries off – they can set aside the thought and come back to it later, or decide not to care about it.

For anxiety victims, this is impossible. Small things might grow in your mind and plague you for hours or more. You might worry constantly about what the future holds, or things you've done in the past. Challenges other people may see as small can be huge to you. Uncertainty cannot be tolerated – for example, if someone tells you they need to talk to you tomorrow, this can trigger panic. What do they want to talk about? Is it bad? Did you do something? This train of thought continues and spirals into worse and worse scenarios, and you experience the mental and physical symptoms of anxiety until the conversation finally happens.

You might experience all or some of what we've talked about, but no matter what, your anxiety is impacting your life. The only way to improve is to treat it. Ignoring it will only make it worse. Fortunately, you can get started just by reading this book. You don't have the obstacle of making a medical appointment or talking to someone about your issues. You can deal with them on your own.

Chapter 2: Social Anxiety and Phobias

"No one can make you feel inferior without your consent." – Eleanor Roosevelt

One of the huge parts of anxiety can be phobias, which are defined as irrational fears. You've probably heard of things like arachnophobia, the fear of spiders, or claustrophobia, the fear of enclosed spaces. Those and other common terms are used to describe average fears pretty often.

However, a true phobia is not based in reason. A

fear of spiders can be rational – you might be afraid of being bitten by a venomous spider, and therefore avoid ones that look dangerous. Even a general fear of the creepy way they look isn't quite a phobia if you can still coexist with spiders. With arachnophobia, the fear doesn't quite have anything to do with a specific attribute of the spiders. It's just there. At a low level, it can cause panic just at the sight of a spider.

At more intense levels, the thought of a spider being in a room may make you avoid it, or the sight of one could cause a full-blown panic attack. Severe enough phobias can be completely debilitating. To be considered a phobia, the fear must last for six months or longer and have a significant effect on your life.

Let's talk about some of the most common phobias. See if any sound familiar to you and if you suffer from any of the symptoms. A phobia can develop for any object or situation, but most people reportedly suffer from one of these. You might be able to relate to one or more of them.

Mysophobia

You've probably heard this one colloquially referred to as germaphobia. It's the fear of dirt, bacteria, germs, and general contamination from these. Sufferers may wash their hands or bathe excessively. They'll often find themselves unable to touch or interact with certain things they consider too dirty. They might keep a large amount of disinfectants and cleansers for their hands, and always have some with them.

Agoraphobia

This is a fear of open places, or any space that isn't their home. It may be specific to a certain type of area, such as a shopping mall. People with this phobia will avoid the areas that scare them at all cost. In severe cases, they are unable to leave their home at all.

Trypanophobia

Many people can relate to this phobia, the fear of needles. Shots, blood draws, and any other medical procedure involving needles are avoided at all costs. Sufferers will even skip necessary procedures when they are sick, injured, or at risk. If they have to have something done, they will experience intense feelings of panic and may even lose consciousness. They might have some symptoms from seeing someone else getting an injection or having blood drawn, or even just from discussing it.

Astraphobia

If you've had pets, chances are that you've had one that experienced this phobia. It's the fear of thunder and lightning. It's one of a few that's shared between humans and animals, typically dogs and cats. Victims will become anxious if there's even a small chance of a thunderstorm developing. They'll watch or listen to the weather reports constantly, sometimes obsessively. When it does storm, they'll feel panicky and may try to hide from the thunder and lightning in some way. Being alone may intensify the fear.

Cynophobia

This is the fear of dogs. It is often developed during childhood, either after a traumatic experience with a dog or from hearing stories of such from other people. Sufferers will avoid dogs, and panic if they get too close to one or are surprised by one. Even pictures of dogs may trigger the fear. They may avoid going to someone's house they know have dogs, public spaces where dogs are welcome, or even new areas if there's a chance of a dog being present.

Aerophobia

The fear of flying is another common one. Just the thought of flying makes the sufferer anxious. They'll often avoid journeys that involve air travel. If they must fly, they may have a panic attack. In severe cases, the mere thought of flying might cause an attack.

Acrophobia

This one is the fear of heights. Most people who have this fear get very anxious when they're in an elevated space. Even if it doesn't seem high by other people's standards, it may be enough to make the sufferer nervous. Things like roller coasters are usually out of the question, and in severe cases even being on a high floor of a tall building can cause distress.

Ophidiophobia

This is the fear of snakes. It can be of the snake itself, or a severe fear of the venom from snakes. Research has found this may be the most common phobia, with somewhere up to 1/3 of people having it. The fear extends to pictures or videos of snakes. It tends to be more common in adults than it is in children. Anywhere that could have snakes is carefully avoided, including common areas like gardens where harmless garter snakes may live.

Arachnophobia

We've already discussed this one a bit. It usually applies to other arachnids as well, such as scorpions, or other creatures that look similar to arachnids but fall under a different category, like the daddy long-legs (also known as a harvestman). In bad cases, the victim may have signs of panic at just a spider web or an image of one. They will usually go to great lengths to avoid places where a spider might live, even areas in their own home such as a basement.

All of these phobias are very common, and can be debilitating if severe enough. Many of them interfere with everyday life, while a few can be avoided except in extenuating circumstances. However, there's one more that belongs on the list of most common phobias. It's the one we'll focus on for the rest of this chapter, and one you'll learn to overcome in this book. Out of all the phobias, it is one of the most difficult to deal with and can have the greatest impact on your life.

Social Phobia

Social phobia is sometimes referred to as simply social anxiety, or sometimes social anxiety disorder, though it's more often looked at as a symptom of a more generalized anxiety disorder. Those with social anxiety have a fear of participating in any social situations. This goes past simple shyness – it's a legitimate and crippling fear of the social events.

The idea of speaking to a stranger is terrifying, and they can't stand the thought of being the center of attention for even a moment. They'll often obsess over the thought of having someone notice them doing something unusual or embarrassing. Some of the symptoms are excessive sweating, stammering speech, blushing or flushed face, nausea, and/or trembling.

Social anxiety boils down to a fear of rejection by other people – it's an aversion to judgement, negative evaluations, embarrassment, and any other sign of not being accepted by other people. Being seen as unintelligent, silly, awkward, or boring are some of the worst things that can happen to victims. They'll go out of their way to avoid this.

This might mean avoiding social situations in general, or specific ones they feel the most vulnerable in. Public performance or speaking is one common trigger. This facet of anxiety typically sets in during the teenage years, though it can show up earlier in childhood or develop in adulthood.

You may have been told at some point in your life, especially when you were young, that you were shy. However, there's a big difference between shyness and social anxiety, and if you've picked up this book you probably have the latter. Shyness is usually being quiet and not talking to others much, or being slightly reluctant to try new social situations.

However, these people are usually comfortable being shy, or can easily make themselves be more outgoing. It's not something that hinders them greatly. They do not have the same avoidance of judgement or embarrassment. They are simply quieter than most.

Some shy people may have social anxiety, and vice versa, but one does not necessarily mean the other. In fact, a lot of people that know they have anxiety rather than shyness do not consider themselves shy at all. This is because they have the desire to get out more and relate to others, but their irrational fear is what stops them.

They might even be talkative and outgoing if they find a social situation they're comfortable in, such as a conversation with a close friend or two. They often recognize their fear is irrational, but are unable to control it. This feeling of not having any control adds to the anxiety.

Social anxiety can cause fear in any social situation, or only in certain ones. Some specific scenarios could be being introduced to new people, being teased or joked about, being the center of attention, being watched while doing something, meeting important people (such as those in a position of authority), having to speak in a group, and interactions with friends or romantic relationships. This is only a handful of potential triggers. Social phobia can be unique between people, so a lot of sufferers probably experience different combinations of these fears.

Unfortunately, social anxiety is very difficult to understand for people who don't have it. Even people in your life who care deeply about you and have good intentions may say dismissive or hurtful things. They don't do it on purpose – they just conflate "shy" with "anxious." That's where phrases like, "don't worry," "just relax," "you'll be fine," and "it's not a big deal" come from. For a person who doesn't understand the social phobia, they think they're being helpful by pointing out what is obvious or comforting to them. However, the victim already knows these things and just has no control over their reaction.

Chapter 3: What Causes Anxiety?

"Learn from the past, set vivid, detailed goals for the future, and live in the only moment over which you have any control: now." – Denis Waitley

While it's hard to pin anxiety on any one cause, there are a lot of ideas behind it. In most cases, it's probably caused by a complicated combination of factors. We'll discuss some of them here, and you might be able to identify with some of them. Most of your treatment will focus on what you're currently feeling. However, it can give some peace of mind to know where a disorder comes from, or at least know you aren't "crazy."

Anxiety has been shown to appear when suffering from some health issues. In some cases, anxiety might even be the first symptom of another illness. If you visit your doctor to discuss your anxiety, they'll likely run some tests for underlying physical issues. Some problems frequently linked to anxiety include heart disease, diabetes, thyroid issues, respiratory disorders (including asthma), drug or alcohol abuse and/or withdrawal, withdrawal from certain prescription medications, chronic pain, irritable bowel syndrome, and some rare tumors that disturb the fight-or-flight hormones. Anxiety also shows up as a side effect for some medications.

How can you tell if one of these illnesses is causing your anxiety? Be on the lookout for any physical symptoms besides the ones directly caused by your anxiety, and see a doctor if you notice anything off. You might have an underlying medical condition if you don't have any immediate family members with anxiety, you weren't anxious as a child, you don't have any phobias, or you have a sudden onset of anxiety that doesn't seem related to an event and despite having no previous history.

Significant or drawn out build-ups of stress can lead to anxiety. When you're stressed for a prolonged period of time, it wears down your body and messes with your fight-or-flight response. Sustaining high stress levels has been shown to lead to generalized anxiety disorder. It could come from one large event, or a string of smaller situations. Having a severe or long-term illness also causes a great deal of stress that can grow into an anxiety disorder.

Environmental factors are often contributors to high stress levels. This could be a difficult personal relationship, a job you hate, difficulty in school, a bad financial situation, or living in an area with a lot of crime. Even the physical environment can lead to anxiety disorders, like the low oxygen levels for people living in high-altitude areas.

Substance abuse can be a huge contributing factor for anxiety. Drugs and alcohol change all sorts of things within your body, both mentally and physically. Using them excessively can lead to anxiety disorders and other mental health issues. However, some people turn to illicit substances to deal with their anxiety they already have. The abuse then produces more anxiety, creating a painful cycle that's difficult to break.

Research has found that anxiety may be linked to genetics. It's still being studied, but it appears that anxiety conditions could be passed down through families. If you have a blood relative who suffers from anxiety, you could have a higher chance of having it yourself. Anxiety in immediate family members does not guarantee you'll have it, though.

Newer studies show your personality type may make you more likely to have anxiety. People who were perfectionists or high-strung as children are more likely to have an anxiety disorder than other personality types. Your personality is influenced by how you learn to interact with the world around you. Some of this is taught to you by others, and some is learned on your own through experience. People who are timider and have lower self-esteem often have anxiety.

Mental health disorders often come in batches. Depression and anxiety are often partners, and one can contribute to the other developing. The coexisting disorders will feed into each other, making treatment more difficult. It's important to treat any mental illnesses you may have, so you lower the risk of developing more that aggravates the situation. General anxiety disorder can also become obsessive compulsive disorder, which is the most severe form of anxiety.

Sometimes you'll hear that your brain chemistry is what causes anxiety and other mental illnesses.

This is still being studied, but anti-anxiety medication typically works by altering the chemicals your brain produces. It's unknown why these delicate balances break, though. It could be because of any of the reasons above, or perhaps a person could be born with a faulty brain. Mental illness disrupts hormones and electrical signals in the brain, but it's a chicken-and-egg scenario – do the imbalances cause the disease, or did the disease cause the imbalance?

Somewhat related to the other factors above, trauma is considered one of the biggest contributors to anxiety disorders. It can happen at any point in your life, but often the biggest focus is placed on those that happened as a child. Children are still learning how the world works, and being shaped by their environment and experiences. If they have the unfortune to be involved in a terrible incident, they'll develop otherwise unusual coping mechanisms that will stick with them for life if not treated.

Traumatic events for a child can include

abandonment, abuse, and neglect. Sometimes the child subconsciously disconnects from their own emotions, tries to overcompensate for their perceived faults, or hides their distress until it eventually manifests as physical illnesses and diseases. If the scenario is one that reoccurs, it solidifies the child's coping mechanism and further roots it in their mind. The anticipation of waiting for the next incident is a huge contributor to anxiety.

Children can be traumatized by any event that disrupts their perceived safety. When humans are young, they have to rely on others to take care of them, and they know they can't survive on their own until they're much older. If something happens to take away their caregiver, shelter, or feeling of safety, they have to develop psychological methods of coping.

Psychological damage can be caused by one-time events like accidents, injuries, or attacks, particularly if they were unexpected. It could also be caused by ongoing stress, perhaps from living in a high crime area, fighting a chronic or life-threatening illness, or repeated traumas like bullying, domestic violence, or neglect.

These are only a few examples of potential causes. There are many that are overlooked as well – surgeries when very young, a sudden death of someone close to the child, the end of a relationship that was a large part of their life, or a deeply embarrassing or disappointing situation. Huge events such as natural or manmade disasters can also disturb a child's sense of safety, even if they weren't directly involved and are only hearing about it on the news.

Studies have found that adults suffering from social anxiety disorder report more childhood trauma than any other form of mental illness. Emotional abuse and neglect were the most widely reported traumas. Overprotective parents can contribute to adult anxiety as well, as their children are forced to learn similar coping mechanisms to otherwise abused or neglected children.

As adults, many say that their parents used shame as a form of punishment, lacked emotional warmth, used insults and swearing, belittled their children, and used other non-physical forms of aggression. These forms of emotional abuse were positively correlated with social anxiety symptoms, and negatively correlated with self-esteem levels. They forced the children to develop coping mechanisms while also lowering their sense of self-worth.

If a child receives prompt and proper care for their trauma, they will be able to heal. As any many other health issues, children tend to be more resilient than adults. However, in cases of emotional abuse or neglect, the child will rarely receive treatment. If it is a close family member who is inflicting the trauma, they won't be the one to seek care for the child.

Some of the immediate symptoms of trauma stand out to others. They can vary widely among children, but they might fear being separated from their parents, cry or scream often, have

39

nightmares, show early signs of anxiety, be fearful more often than others, and have difficulty concentrating. Trauma survivors are more likely to experience learning disabilities, worse physical health, increased interactions with juvenile justice or child welfare systems, and have long-term health problems.

If a child is brought in for treatment, there are different methods available depending on the child, their reactions, and their needs. Cognitive behavioral therapy is just as widely used as it is with adults, and often shows fast results. Talk therapy is sometimes used, but a lot of traumatized children can't or won't talk to a professional. Medication might rarely be used, but usually only in severe cases. Using psychological medicine in children does not have a great deal of research yet, and long-term effects are unknown. Side effects can be worse in children as well.

Without proper treatment before developing into an adult, the unresolved feelings of fear and helplessness stick around. Because of this, they're more susceptible to further trauma. Their self-esteem and resilience are low. The anxiety that trauma causes also prevents them from speaking out, or seeking help. They may not even realize they have a problem, since their behavior was normal to them as a child. While the exact link between childhood trauma and adult social anxiety is still being studied, it's clear that there is a connection, and that past abuse makes it harder to treat as an adult.

Chapter 4: Introduction to CBT

"The secret of getting ahead is getting started."

– Agatha Christie

Cognitive behavioral therapy, also known as CBT, is a combination of cognitive and behavioral psychotherapies that focuses on changing the way the brain interacts with information. It was developed by the psychiatrist Aaron Beck in the 1960s. As he was treating patients with depression, he noticed the connection between their mental illness and negative thoughts.

His patients were having what he called "automatic thoughts," or instant reactions to situations based on incorrect beliefs or assumptions. These could be caused by a past experience or a false belief brought on by the depression. Almost everyone experiences automatic thoughts, but with mental illness, they have a greater impact and are harder to dismiss.

Today, CBT is one of the most studied forms of therapy. It has been proven to be highly effective for anxiety, depression, and addiction. In fact, it is sometimes just as effective, if not more effective than using medication alone. Unlike other forms of therapy, CBT does not focus on talking or events in the patient's past. It centers around the thoughts, feelings, and actions the person is currently experiencing, regardless of

43

their initial cause. The goal is to change your thoughts and feelings, which in turn changes your behavior. If one of the things in that cycle is negative, they all will be, creating a loop of negativity that feeds into anxiety and depression.

CBT is often done by working with a therapist for a relatively short amount of time. Typically, you'll find a therapist who specializes in CBT. However, it can be done on your own. We'll go over how you can do this in the next chapter. The benefits of having a therapist is you get an outside perspective – they can identify things you may miss when looking at yourself, and they can provide additional guidance if necessary.

Working on your own, though, gives you flexibility, extra customization, and additional privacy. Even though therapists listen to people as their job and keep everything confidential, sometimes talking to a stranger about your problems can inhibit some of what you say, even subconsciously.

The idea of the cycle between thoughts, feelings, and actions is the basis for CBT. When the brain receives information, it instantly processes it to see if the body is in danger or not. The brain is very complex, but it will take shortcuts whenever it can to keep everything running smoothly. This means it will take information from previous experiences or already held ideas to process what it is currently experiencing.

This is where the negative automatic thoughts can create a problem. The brain doesn't check to see if these things are true or not, it just presents the thoughts. You then feel emotions based on these thoughts. In the case of automatic thoughts, they are usually negative emotions. Your feelings then inform the actions you take. Negative feelings will make you take defensive or ill-advised actions, while positive feelings will help you get through the situation with little difficulty.

Your behavior also reinforces your thoughts. Positive reactions reaffirm to your mind the minimal impact of the negative trigger. However, negative reactions will confirm the negative thoughts to your brain. Even if the negative thoughts aren't true or based in reality, your brain will still believe you're confirming them and it will use these experiences to inform your future thoughts. It's building more of those shortcuts in your brain.

Many of the physical symptoms that accompany anxiety make positive behaviors more difficult to engage in. For example, fatigue will prevent you from exercising, and cause you to lay in bed more. Since your thoughts, feelings, and actions form a cycle, any negative actions or lack of positive actions will feed the negative thoughts and feelings. It's difficult to break this cycle. However, you'll notice an improvement the moment that you do. Even improving just one part of the circle will help the others heal. CBT focuses on the thoughts first.

As a simple example, let's say you've spilled a glass of juice. Without negative automatic thoughts getting in the way, you'll simply clean up the spill and pour yourself a new glass, and likely not think of the accident again. However, when dealing with anxiety, the automatic thoughts will pop up as soon as the glass tips over. You may find yourself thinking things such as, "I can't believe I'm so clumsy," or "What a mess, I'll never get this cleaned up."

These will create negative feelings – frustration, anger, guilt, even despair. Then, that informs your actions. Perhaps you'll clean up the spill, but put your glass away instead of refilling it, and the accident will come back to mind throughout the rest of your day. Or, you may not clean up the mess at all, opting to simply not deal with it. That will lead to further problems, like stains and stickiness, that you'll have to deal with later. It becomes a cycle that's hard to break.

That example may seem extreme, but it illustrates the connection between thoughts, feelings, and actions, and how warped our perception can become if we're used to choosing the negative options. Because of the negative thoughts, the situation suddenly seemed like a much bigger deal that would be difficult to clean up and handle.

When you suffer from depression, these small tasks can seem insurmountable. The spill will sit and stain the table it's on, and the rest of the coffee in the pot in the kitchen will go cold and need scrubbed out. Now the problem has increased and is even harder to take care of. That brings on more negative thoughts and feelings, and actions that just lead to further issues. That's the cycle of depression.

It's natural to experience negative thoughts and emotions sometimes. However, those with mental disorders like anxiety and depression experience them more often and more intensely. Any person could benefit from clearing out some of their negative thoughts, but it's imperative for someone with anxiety. When you are anxious, the bad incidents stand out much more than the good ones.

To be healthy, you'll learn to experience normal negative emotions without letting them dictate your actions and behavior. It takes time and work to get to that point. Once you do, you'll see that a bad day won't destroy your mood anymore, and it will be easier to forgive yourself for mistakes and move on.

CBT works by getting rid of the negative thoughts that aren't based in reality. Anxiety can bring a lot of pessimism and even depression with it, and sufferers will often have a lot of negative self-talk. This leads to a poor view of the world around them. This feeds into that cycle of bad things. CBT breaks this cycle, and exposes the lies your brain tells you for what they are. You'll learn to replace them with truth and positivity, and you might even find yourself becoming an optimist.

We talked some earlier about how anxiety physically works in the brain, and the shortcuts your brain uses to inform your reactions. These shortcuts are actually literal – your brain creates new neural pathways when it makes connections between two things. CBT actually helps to redirect these pathways.

As you begin to challenge negative automatic thoughts and see new positive aspects of your life, the paths will change and new ones will be created. This has even more benefits than a more positive outlook on life. Teaching your brain to make new pathways makes it easier to do so in the future, which translates to higher intellect and a better memory.

The first step of CBT is simply identifying your negative thoughts. There are several categories that they can fall under, which we'll go over in the next chapter. Once you can successfully recognize the automatic thoughts, you'll begin to challenge them by applying logic and taking away assumptions.

Finally, you'll replace these negative thoughts with positive ones. The steps sound fairly simple, though they can be hard at first. Learning which of your thoughts are false automatic ones can change the way you look at things. Even if this is a good thing, it is difficult and has a huge impact on your life.

To get the most out of this book and help with your CBT, you'll need to start a journal. That may not sound fun if you don't typically write or have never kept a journal. However, it can actually be a powerful tool for your recovery. It might take some time to get into the habit of writing in it, but it won't be long until you're doing it every day. Once you are, you'll see an improvement in your mental state.

You can keep your journal in any way you choose. You can find hundreds of types of notebooks, journals, and sketchbooks at any store. You can buy a new one, use an old one you already have at home, or even bind your own if you're crafty. You can find digital options too, in the form of apps or simply a word processing program.

Handwriting your journal has been shown to be more beneficial, but if having it digitally means you'll write in it regularly, that's more important. Pick the method and style that suits your preferences best. The idea is to have something you actually enjoy using, or at the very least don't hate.

This journal will be for your eyes only. Don't let anyone else see it, just like the diaries with little locks that girls keep in grade school. If you have it in your head that someone else could read it, you'll subconsciously edit what you write and won't be as honest and open as you should be.

Keep the journal in a safe place where no one will accidentally come across it. When it's time to write, pick a quiet and private place where no one can interrupt you or read over your shoulder. Find yourself the freedom to write whatever you need to without the possibility of anyone else judging it.

You can also use your journal as a way to track your progress. As you work on your mental health, you can flip back to old entries and see the difference in your state of mind. Once you set some goals and start working towards them, you'll see the progress that you've made in a visual form. That's awesome motivation. Even if you're having a bad day, looking back at how far you've come since starting will boost you up. You'll have physical proof in front of you that you are capable of improving, and you can continue to do so.

If you've never journaled before, or just haven't in a long time, it might help to start building the habit before you get started on CBT. Practice writing for just a few minutes each day. Get acquainted with the journal you've selected, and experiment to find the right time and place for you. You can create an account of your day, write down whatever thoughts you currently have, or even just jot down a little story or piece of an idea that you want to get down. This helps you get used to the idea of writing exactly what's on your mind. That will give you a head start when it's time to start writing for your CBT.

Besides setting up a journal, the only things you need for CBT are time, space, and the desire to improve. Time is sometimes difficult for us to find. Many people are busy all day, and have a lot going on at any given moment. However, you'll need to set aside time for your therapy. It will arguably be one of the most important things you do in a day.

It's a good idea to set a specific time each day to dedicate to CBT. Write it on a calendar, set an alarm on your phone, and stick to it religiously. After a few weeks, you'll build this into a habit, and will automatically be ready for therapy at that time you chose.

If you are incapable of setting aside any time at all in your day for CBT, it's time to take a hard look at your schedule. You need that time in order to get better. Not only that, but with a day that busy you're going to exhaust yourself if you haven't already. That's bad for both your physical and mental health, and will contribute to your anxiety. If it's work that is taking up a huge amount of time, see if you can work less hours, at least temporarily.

If your time is filled to the brim with personal activities, pick out the ones that mean the most to you, and cut out some of the others. As human beings, we need time to rest and recharge. If you're running yourself ragged, even if it's things you generally enjoy, you can't get that time. Your body and mind both need it.

As for space, this doesn't need to be anything too special. If there's an office or some other work space in your home, you can use that. The most important thing you need is quiet and solitude. That way you can focus on what you need to with minimal distractions. Being alone also means that you can do or write exactly what you need to without fear of someone judging you. If you live with other people and don't have a lot of space to get away, try out your bedroom or somewhere outdoors. It might help to give others a heads up that you need some quiet time, and tell them how long. For the most part, people want to be helpful, so if you ask for help in this they'll likely oblige.

The will to work on your anxiety may be the hardest part. Just by picking up this book, though, you've already taken an important first step. You've acknowledged that you have a problem and that it needs corrected. If someone else recommended this book to you, they probably noticed something about your attitude or health that concerns them. If that's the case, take some time to reflect on what that could be. Either way, look at where you currently are in life, and where you would like to be. You've now formed the basis for your progress.

It should be noted that this book is not medical advice. If you are having difficulty functioning day-to-day or your mood is extremely low, reach out to a professional. Medication is sometimes necessary to balance out the chemicals that your brain produces. CBT can act as a supplement to the medication, and changing the way you think may lead you down a path that lets you come off of medication eventually.

If you have thoughts of harming yourself or others, please seek emergency help immediately. You can call the free National Suicide Prevention Lifeline at 1-800-273-8255 for safe, confidential, non-judgmental help and resources. If you are in immediate danger, call 911.

Chapter 5: Using CBT

"What you do today can improve all your tomorrows." – Ralph Marston

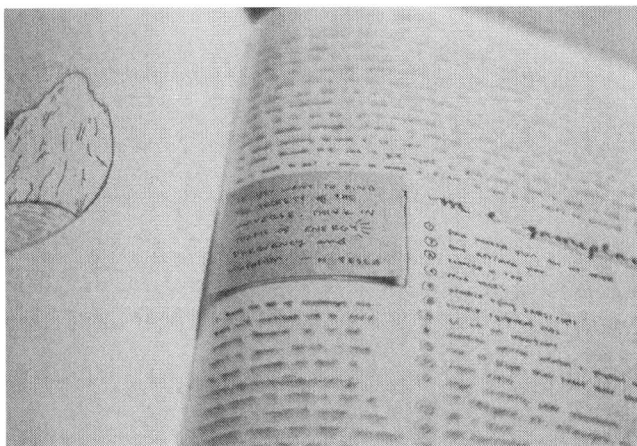

Before you dive into cognitive behavioral therapy, you need to decide what you want to accomplish with it. If you're reading this book, you're probably experiencing the symptoms of anxiety, so your broad goal is to reduce that. However, you'll need to be more specific. Consider what "happiness" looks like to you. How is your anxiety affecting your life, and keeping you from happiness? What could your life look like if you didn't have the stumbling block of anxiety?

The very first section in your journal should be for your goals. It's a good idea to pick one to focus on at the beginning. This can be either a short-term or long-term goal. Either way, you'll be breaking it down into smaller steps that are easy to accomplish. Give yourself a timeline, or a date to reach each step by. You want to set yourself up for success in this regard. Make sure your goals are challenging, but not out of reach. Give yourself plenty of time to reach your stepping stones. Pushing yourself too hard only leads to disappointment and frustration, which will set you back on your path to better mental health. Make sure you have plenty of time and resources to accomplish what you want.

If you chose to work on CBT with the aid of a therapist, they'll typically work with you to create goals relevant to you and reachable with your current resources. Doing it alone presents a bit more of a challenge. It can be hard to make big plans when you're not currently in a healthy state of mind. You might need to dig deep to find that motivation that you need.

Keep in mind though that you don't need to make huge, life-changing goals at the moment. Just consider where you are right now, and where you would like to be. Choose a point that feels realistic to you right now. Set that as your main goal. This can always be changed later – as your mental health improves, you might realize you can be a bit more ambitious. For the moment, however, pick whatever seems reasonable to you right now.

If you find yourself completely stuck on coming up with your goals, start doing some research. Search online for phrases like "therapy goals" or "anxiety goals." You'll find dozens of lists and pages of resources that might give you a starting point. Remember that every person is unique, and you'll find things from people in all points of their recovery journeys.

Make sure your goals are specifically tailored to

you, and reachable with your current mental and physical resources. Be careful not to fall into the trap of comparing yourself to other people, or thinking you need to meet someone else's expectations. It's a great idea to look for inspiration, but you should adjust it for you. Here is a very small set of categories and examples that may give you a jumpstart.

- Financial – Make more money, get out of debt, buy a desired item

- Career – Get your dream job, get promoted, start your own business

- Health – Run a marathon, exercise regularly, eat healthily

- Knowledge – Get a degree, learn a new skill, take classes on a desired subject

- Relationships – Maintain friendships, make new friends, attend a certain number of social events

- Public service – Start a charity, volunteer a certain number of hours, donate money

- Family – Have your desired number of children, be closer to family members, have family nights at set intervals

- Hobbies – Master a skill, learn a new hobby, make an income from your hobby

- Spiritual – Practice your religion, learn about new religions, teach others your views on spiritualism

Business experts came up with an acronym to help them set goals, and more and more people are using it in all sorts of settings. The acronym is SMART, with each letter standing for an aspect of an ideal goal.

- S – Specific. Your goal should be well defined. For example, "get rich" is vague and therefore difficult to make plans towards. Make it more specific, such as "have $50,000 in savings."

- M – Measurable. You should be able to measure and track your progress towards your goal. If your goal is fitness related, one of your steps might be to run more often. Instead of saying "run every week," set it as something like "run every Monday, Wednesday, and Friday." Then you can check off days that you completed your run, and clearly see how well you're doing.

- A – Achievable. Make sure that you can reach your goal with your current resources, or resources you can easily gain. Don't set your goal too far out of your reach, or as something that you can't actually work towards. For example, "win the lottery" is not a good goal right now. It's not something you can definitively achieve or make progress towards. If you're goals aren't actually achievable, you're setting yourself up for disappointment.

- R – Relevant. All of the stepping stone goals you set should be related to your main goal. Skills you gain, opportunities you pursue, or actions you take should be leading up to your big goal. Learning a new language might be a good goal, but it won't get you any closer to your goal of being hired as a chef. For now, you'll need all of your focus on your main goal.

- T – Timely. This applies to a couple of things. First, make sure the time is right to work on your particular goal. As a simple example, starting a butterfly garden is a great goal, but you shouldn't start working towards it at the beginning of winter. If you want to be more physically active, don't set that as your goal right after you've had surgery on your leg. Set goals you can actively work towards right this moment. The second meaning behind being timely is setting yourself certain dates or a timeline to reach your stepping stones by.

In addition to being SMART, your goals should be positive. They should be something that improves your life, and worded in an optimistic way. Working towards the goal of "be less fat" is demoralizing and not good to look at every day. "Be more fit" as a positive alternative to that, and invokes a sense of optimism and future health. The words you use have a huge effect on how you see yourself and the world around you.

To help keep your goals positive and cultivate motivation, write down your reasons for them. Be sure to use positive wording in this, as well – no negative undertones or self insults. Explain why you want to accomplish this specific goal. Describe how it will make your life better. Take some time to visualize your life after reaching your goal, and write that out.

Now that you know what you're working towards, the first step of CBT is learning to identify the automatic thoughts that create negative feelings for you. You'll be writing in your journal for this. To begin, you'll simply keep a log of negative thoughts. Start writing down any time that you experience any. Write down the thought, the situation surrounding it, the emotions you felt, any physical effects it had, and what actions you took. That's all you'll be doing for a while. The idea is to simply acknowledge the negative thoughts you have, and how they affect you in different situations. Just noticing the negativity will make it stand out more to you, and make the next steps easier.

You can set up your journal any way you'd like, but one suggestion is to create a chart. Make a column for the negative thought, the date and time, the scenario you were in, what emotions you experienced, any physical symptoms you noticed, what behaviors or actions you took because of the negative thought, and one for cognitive distortions that you'll fill out in the future. Create several rows in your chart, and have them ready to go for future thought logging.

It likely won't take long, perhaps a few days to a week, but you'll soon realize you can recognize negative reactions you hadn't before. Once you get to this point, it's time to start naming your automatic thoughts. Beck created a list of what he called cognitive distortions, or different categories that automatic thoughts can fall under. The list has been slightly modified and added to over the years, but it has remained largely the same.

Cognitive distortions are always negative and usually exaggerated by your mind. Despite not being based in reality, they can be convincing. After all, if your own mind is saying it, it must be true, right? However, once you examine them closely, you'll see the falsehoods behind them. They do not serve you and only create that negative cycle that feeds your anxiety.

Look over the following list and its examples, and see if you recognize any of the categories in your own thoughts. You might find that you have some thoughts that don't fit neatly into a category. The real test is whether or not it's based on something true, and if it serves any positive purpose.

Black and White Thinking

This may also be referred to as all or nothing thinking or polarized thinking. It is the idea that everything falls on one extreme or another, and there are no in-betweens. It is all black or white, with no shades of grey. This will cause hatred or other strong negative emotions towards anything on the wrong side of the imaginary scale. It also forces you to ignore all of the middle ground, and likely some more reasonable actions or ideas.

Examples

- You either hate or love everyone you know, with no in between

- Believing you're perfect when everything is going well, or a failure when it's not

- A best friend becomes a worst enemy if you're angry with them

Overgeneralization

If something happens once or twice, those with

this cognitive distortion see it as a pattern and a prediction of the future. It ignores all of the nuances that can change a situation to apply assumptions. Broader overgeneralization is also how stereotypes are formed. Because of overgeneralization, you'll expect bad outcomes even with nothing lead to that idea, and feel negative going into various situations.

Examples

- A friend cancels plans at the last minute, so you think they'll never come out with you

- You failed a test in school, so you think you'll fail the next one

- Your boss addresses some small mistakes with you, so you're convinced you'll make more and lose your job

Mental Filter

The mental filter causes you to ignore positive things, and focus only on negatives. If a critique of some sort is given, the positive aspects of it won't be noticed at all, and the negative will be taken to heart. Oftentimes the person with this distortion won't notice the positives at all. It can cause low self-esteem and discouragement.

Examples

- When your boss gives you a review at work, you only hear the negative comments and can't remember any of the positive ones later

- You and your significant other disagree on one thing so you think the relationship is ending, even though you get along well otherwise

- You ask a friend for their opinion on something you're working on, but only focus on the negative comments

Discounting the Positive

Like the mental filter, the person with this distortion focuses on the negative aspects of everything. However, they still notice the positives, but believe them to be false or exaggerated. This is one of the tougher cognitive distortions to overcome, because even providing evidence to the contrary of the person's beliefs may not help. It leads to self-doubt, self-criticism, and low motivation.

Examples

- You receive a positive yearly review at work, but believe it's only positive to keep you from quitting and making them find a replacement

- When you receive compliments, you assume the person is just being nice rather than actually meaning it

- When receiving a critique on a project you've worked on, you only believe the negative comments, and think the positive ones are only there to soften the blow

Mind Reading

This is jumping to conclusions about what others think or feel based on little to no evidence. It is referred to as "mind reading" because the person with this distortion believes they know what is going on in someone else's mind. More often than not, they think it is something negative about them. It can make social situations difficult, and cause the sufferer to question the motivations of everyone around them.

Examples

- Your teacher scowls slightly when you hand in a test, so you think she's seen something bad on it and you're going to fail

- A stranger near you starts laughing, and you immediately think it's at your expense

- The person at the next table over in a restaurant briefly frowns at you, so you think you've done something to offend them

Fortune Telling

This is another way to jump to conclusions, but by predicting the outcome of situations without any evidence. This is almost always in a negative manner. It forces you to focus on one bad outcome, without exploring the possibility of any others. It can take the joy out of doing things, and bring on fear of trying new experiences.

Examples

- Your friend asks you to go see a movie you haven't heard of, but you think it will be bad, so you decline

- You believe your significant other is going to cancel your date night, even though they've made no indication of this

- There are a few clouds in the sky, so you think your outdoor party is going to be ruined by rain

Catastrophizing

This cognitive distortion is one of the greatest contributors to anxiety. It is similar to fortune telling, but also inflates small negative aspects to make them much more significant. It latches on to anything negative and extrapolates it into something bigger.

Examples

- Your friend hasn't answered your last couple of texts, so you think they're no longer speaking to you

- A glass figurine you just bought is broken, and you think there's no way you'll be able to replace it even though the store had several in stock

- You make a small mistake at work and can't think about anything else the rest of the day, waiting for someone to yell at you for it

Minimizing

This goes along with catastrophizing, but it's when you reduce the impact of something positive in order to support a negative belief. Just as catastrophizing inflates the negative, minimizing reduces the positive.

Examples

- You receive a raise at work, but since it isn't very large, you still believe you're doing poorly despite other evidence

- Your friend misses a few of your calls and then returns one, so you think they don't want to speak with you and only returned one to get you to stop annoying them

- You receive high marks on a school project, but believe it can't make up for how poorly you've done leading up to then

Emotional Reasoning

This is a very common cognitive distortion, even in people not suffering from a mental illness. It is the idea that because you feel it, it is true. Usually we can recognize that just because we feel a certain emotion, doesn't mean it's justified. However, with emotional reasoning, you feel that you are correct and there is no other way to feel in the current scenario.

Examples

- You are mad at a friend, so you believe they definitely did something wrong even if others don't think so

- You get a sense of dread while at home alone, so you believe something bad is certainly going to happen

- You feel sad and hopeless, so you don't think there is any way to solve your problems

Should Statements

These are thoughts that often include words like "should," "must," "ought," and so on. It is when you tell yourself that you *should* do something or *should* have done something a certain way. These types of thought aren't productive as their purpose isn't to reflect on different options, but to guilt you into selecting certain ones.

It limits your options and stops you from seeing others. It also brings on guilt if you didn't do something the way you *should* have, or dread about having to do something a certain way and disappointment if you can't. It is also applied to others and scenarios, leading to strict expectations that usually aren't met.

Examples

- You feel you must lose weight in order to be attractive

- You believe you should have started a project sooner to have gotten it done on time

- Your friend called to cancel dinner at the last minute, and you feel they should have contacted you earlier

Labeling

This is applying a broad label to something or someone based on one aspect. We apply these to ourselves as well as others. It is used to judge value based on little information to support it. Applying negative labels to yourself lowers self-esteem and creates more negative automatic thoughts based on them. Putting these labels on others can lead to misjudgment or unrealistic expectations.

Examples

- Calling yourself stupid for making a mistake

- Labeling a friend as "rude" for saying something small in a moment of anger

- Deciding that your boss is a jerk after giving you feedback

Personalization

This is the belief that you are the center of attention in any given situation. This can sound selfish, but it's more typically applied in a negative way. Things are taken personally despite evidence to the contrary, and blame is taken for anything bad that happens. It leads to guilt, unhappiness, and discouragement towards social situations.

Examples

- Your date didn't like the restaurant you took them out to, so you blame yourself and assume they don't like you

- Your friend is in a bad mood, so you assume you did something to cause it

- A company-wide email is sent out at work with a reminder about breakroom rules, and you believe it's because of one small mistake you made a couple of weeks ago

Control Fallacy

This is either the belief you have no control over your life, or complete control over your life. For the first one, control is contributed to other people, outside forces, or something like "fate," and creates the idea that you shouldn't try to control anything in your life since you can't make any difference. The latter creates the idea absolutely everything can be controlled by you, so anything bad that happens is your fault and you hold yourself accountable for the happiness of others.

Examples

- You blame mistakes at work on your boss not training you, even though they did

- Your friend is going through something difficult, and you consider it your responsibility to fix it

- You believe everything falls to fate, so there's no point in trying to do better for yourself

Fallacy of Fairness

All of us would like to believe life is fair, but it obviously isn't. The fallacy of fairness is demanding that everything be fair, and experiencing resentment, anger, and hurt when it isn't. In reality, life is too complicated to boil down to a basic idea of fairness.

Examples

- Your sister hasn't paid you back $5 you let her borrow, so you think it's okay to take $5 out of her purse without telling her

- You didn't receive recognition for every bit of your contribution to a project at work, making you bitter and angry

- You ask to take time off work equal to some overtime you put in, and are angry when your boss says that isn't the policy

Fallacy of Change

This often comes with the belief that your happiness lies in the hands of others. Because of that, you might expect them to make changes specifically for your benefit, regardless of how it affects them. This can have a large negative impact on your social life. Others might view you as selfish or even controlling.

Examples

- You think your friend should cancel plans they've already made to go out with you

- You believe if your significant other did things for you more often, you'd be able to treat them better and be happier

- You feel you can't be happy if you don't have a certain amount of social time each week

Perfectionism

You've probably heard of this distortion before. It's the idea you must always be right, and that being wrong is the worst failure you can experience. People with this distortion will often hold their own opinions as fact, and disregard evidence that contradicts them. They will argue and fight to be right, often at the expense of others. They are typically seen as overly combative, unfriendly, and a "know-it-all." It makes it difficult to maintain healthy relationships with others.

Examples

- People online who argue over something well past the point of reason

- Arguing with your spouse about who does what chores, and refusing to compromise

- Becoming angry and arguing when someone presents facts that prove your opinion wrong

<u>Magical Thinking</u>

This is the idea that good things will happen for you once you reach a certain goal. That is true to a certain degree, but this is considered magical thinking because everything will "magically" be better as soon as that point is reached. Statements in thoughts are usually similar to, "Everything will be better once I _____," or "If I _____, I will get _____." This leads to frustration, anger, and disappointment when the goal is reached but the magical result doesn't appear. It can also cause you to set goals that are too lofty and unreachable.

Examples

- "When I lose twenty pounds, I'll find the man I want to marry."

- "As soon as I get a new job, I'll be happier and richer and everything will come together."

- "My life will be so much better once I'm rich."

Heaven's Reward Fallacy

You may have heard of the idea of "karma" before. The Heaven's Reward fallacy is a similar concept. It is the belief that any act of selflessness, self-sacrifice, or hard work will be rewarded positively. This might be immediately by your peers or others, or in the future in the afterlife. The distortion most strongly applies to

84

the idea of rewards in the near future, however. The person suffering from this will give up happiness and their own desires, and then expect an appropriate reward for it. In addition to making them immediately unhappy, they will be frustrated, disappointed, and bitter when their reward isn't received.

Examples

- You believe that by working more overtime than anyone else you will get a larger raise

- You sign up as a volunteer in a soup kitchen with the idea of a karmic reward, rather than to help the cause

- You believe that setting aside your own life to help a friend with their problems means they will do the same for you in the near future

Double Standard

This is when you hold yourself to a higher standard than everyone else. Even though you believe a certain standard is okay for others to meet, you feel the need to exceed it. It's a way of comparing yourself to others and often sees you creating an unrealistically high bar for yourself that you don't expect anyone else to reach.

Examples

- You and your friend received a B on the exam. You congratulate your friend, but scold yourself for not getting an A

- You don't judge others for the way they're dressed at work, but worry about whether or not you look nice enough

- You tell your colleague it's no big deal that they're a couple of days behind on their project, but are upset with yourself for not getting yours done early

Keep a list of cognitive distortions handy and reference it often. As you write down your negative thoughts, list what cognitive distortions apply to them. You might have some thoughts that fit more than one of the distortions. Write all of them. This stage of CBT is acknowledging and naming your automatic thoughts. Calling them what they are takes away some of their power. Think of fairy tales in which knowing a character's name gives power over them – that concept is based in reality. Picking out your negative thoughts and naming them makes them less vague and threatening. They become a specific thing your mind can easily deal with.

Continue writing down your thoughts and the distortions that apply to them for a week or two. As time goes on, you'll notice you're catching automatic thoughts almost immediately and can identify them easily. The more you practice, the easier this will become.

Once you can recognize the cognitive distortions that pop into your head, you can start challenging them. You'll know you're ready when you can name the distortion without much effort. You're going to start writing in your journal exactly why your negative thoughts aren't true or useful to you. This is usually called cognitive restructuring, or cognitive reframing.

Stick to keeping your log of negative thoughts. You're going to start adding to the information you record about them. It's helpful to do this as soon as possible, so the scenario is still fresh in your mind. At the very least, make sure you do it the same day. Waiting until the next day means it won't be as prominent in your mind, and it will be harder to dissect. To pick apart your negative thoughts, consider the following questions.

- **Is it true?** This is the most important question to answer, and with cognitive distortions, the answer will almost always be no. However, pointing that out to yourself is helpful and erases any doubt you may have had. Automatic thoughts are based in assumptions, opinions, or beliefs. Even though these can be faulty, we typically accept our own thoughts as facts.

Differentiate between facts and opinions in your thoughts, and consider any opinions with a grain of salt. Also look for thoughts that are based on someone else's opinions, especially if that person isn't reliable to begin with.

- **Is it useful?** Does your thought give you any new information, or shed light on something productive? Weight the costs and benefits of considering this automatic thought. More often than not, there are going to be more costs, and in that case, you can discard it. If you find there are several benefits, consider why. You might find something else you'd like to work on, even though it's worded in a harmful way. Most distortions are not productive, however.

- **Does evidence support it?** Take a look at your negative thought and the situation surrounding it as objectively as you can. It can help to imagine you're in a courtroom.

Consider what evidence the defense attorney can provide in favor of the thought. They have to be facts, though – statements like "I feel..." or "It looks like..." and other similar ones will not be accepted. Next, play out the prosecuting attorney's part in arguing against the thought. Again, only use facts. Finally, you'll be the judge, and rule whether the thought should be thrown out or not. It probably will be.

- **What are the alternatives?** Think of different ways you could have viewed the scenario that triggered an automatic thought. Look for the good in the situation, and brainstorm some positive or at least neutral thoughts that would work better. Also consider how the situation might have played out if you didn't have that negative thought. Would it have changed the way you saw it? Would you have taken different actions?

- **What's the worst possible outcome?** This is particularly useful for anxiety, since it's usually rooted in a fear of the future. Consider the situation that previously or currently is making you anxious, and imagine the worst way it could play out. In most situations, you'll realize it's actually not as bad as you thought. Showing yourself that the scenario wouldn't be terrible can calm your anxiety.

- **Am I missing the middle ground?** It's important to ask this no matter what, but particularly if you suffer from all-or-nothing thinking. If you find yourself only considering two possible outcomes, one quite bad and the other very good, you're probably missing out on the gray areas in between. Life is too complex to boil down to black or white, and doing so severely limits your perspective. Consider which possibilities might fall in the middle, and right them down in your journal. You might even create a scale with one of your original thoughts on one end, and the other on the opposite. Fill in the space between them, working up from the bad situations and gradually coming to the good.

Challenging your negative thoughts in your journal will show you that your distortions are nothing more than just that – they are not based in reality, and you now have proof of that. Practice challenging your thoughts as often as you can. As you get better at it, it will come easier and easier, until you find yourself challenging the thoughts as soon as you have them. Keep up on your thought log, and add these challenges to it.

You can also challenge some of your negative thoughts by turning them into questions. Take any statements that place a limit on you, such as "This is too hard," or "I can't make it." Obviously, these are negative and harmful thoughts to have. Make them work for you by changing them into questions – "How can I make this easier?" and

"How can I make it?" You're immediately making them less negative, and instead making them the beginning to solving a problem. It creates the path for eliminating the obstacles you're facing. It's a small thing to do, but it can completely change the way you view a situation.

After you're comfortable challenging your negative thoughts, it's time to start replacing them with positive ones. Some of your distortions may have lessened or become less frequent at this point, simply from naming them and fighting against them. For the ones that remain, you're going to learn to change them to something good.

Take a look back at your negative thought log. Are there any patterns? You might have some thoughts that come up again and again, or a recurring topic that bothers you. Start a new list in your journal and write down these reoccurring topics. Next to each one, you'll counter it or reword it with a positive spin. You want to drastically reduce the negativity without straying too far from the original thought.

You aren't dismissing these thoughts, as they are clearly important to your brain and ignoring them won't do much good. Instead, you're figuring out how to look at them differently. If you try to counter them with something that's too far-fetched, your mind simply won't believe you.

Keep noting down your negative thoughts, but practice opposing them all with positive statements. If you find your better statements getting repetitive, make sure you change up the wording or idea somewhat. Avoid it becoming a rote thing that you automatically write down every day without thinking. Bit by bit, increase the amount of positivity in your counter arguments. As you challenge more of your distortions and dismiss them, you'll find it easier to see the bright side of things.

Look back at the situations you've written about in your journal that have triggered automatic negative thinking. What positives can you find in each one? Not just the ones that are direct counters to your negativity, but any and all good things. Even in a bad situation, there may be some advantage gained, like a lesson learned or new knowledge learned. Even if you can only find one thing that's positive, write it down.

Chapter 6: Practicing Mindfulness

"The present moment is filled with joy and happiness. If you are attentive, you will see it." –
Thich Nhat Hanh

The key to soothing your immediate anxiety is to get the amygdala to calm down. It's working hard to keep your body ready for a threat, even though there isn't actually one present. One method of calming your mind is to practice mindfulness.

Mindfulness for stress and anxiety calls for compassion for yourself, while developing a safe and healthy distance between yourself and the anxiety. It allows you to step back, examine your feelings, and choose how to deal with them.

What is mindfulness? You've likely heard the phrase, but may not be sure what exactly it is. Essentially it is the practice of purposefully paying attention to the present moment. It's taking a step back to view your current state as objectively and non-judgmentally as possible. Instead of listening to your amygdala's fear response, you'll tune in to your thoughts, feelings, and physical sensations. You'll learn to ground yourself in the face of stress, making your anxiety more manageable from day to day.

Mindfulness is our ability to be fully present in the moment, aware of where we are and what we're doing, without being reactive or overwhelmed. It's something that everyone can do, but consciously practicing it cultivates it into a powerful tool. Mindfulness reduces stress, enhances performance, gives valuable insights, and raises awareness.

While the idea of mindfulness is becoming more mainstream, there are still many misconceptions surrounding it. It is sometimes viewed as being mystical or something to be skeptical of, but it's just a naturally occurring awareness you're heightening. It doesn't require you to make any changes to yourself or your life.

It isn't a special skill or ability that only certain people can unlock. Anyone can do it with no prior knowledge or background. However, it does become a way of life. As you practice mindfulness, you'll find yourself noticing more of your surroundings and the things you feel. It will open your eyes to new experiences, and give you the ability to take small pauses throughout the day to recharge.

Scientifically, meditation has been shown to lower breathing, pulse rate, and blood pressure, all things that spike when anxiety is high.

Extensive studies have shown that anxiety conditions are greatly reduced by practicing regular mindfulness meditation. Depressive thoughts are lower after meditation. More and more studies are being done all the time, and proving mindfulness and meditation are beneficial to body and mind.

When practicing mindfulness, you'll take control of your brain rather than letting it run on auto-pilot. The amygdala wants you to act on your fear, but instead, you're going to view it as an outsider. It can be helpful to think of yourself as the sky, and your thoughts and emotions as clouds. You can watch the clouds drift by, but the sky will always be in its place.

When learning mindful meditation, the easiest thing to focus on is your breath. When you're anxious, your breath comes faster and shallower to accommodate the fight-or-flight response. Normally, the breathing would slow and become deeper again once the threat is gone. By focusing on your breath, you'll force it into that calmer state. To start out, you can simply close your eyes and direct your attention to your breathing. Focus on slowing the breath. Let it remain natural, while gradually slowing it. This simple concentration will calm down your entire body, and help dampen that fear response that's brining anxiety.

Beyond just focusing on your breath, there are many types of meditations that you can explore. A common one for beginners is the body scan. In addition to paying attention to your breath, you'll notice and acknowledge different sensations throughout your body. It can take about thirty to forty minutes and is very relaxing.

It will build up your ability to be completely in the present moment, your full attention on what's happening right in front of you. In other words, getting out of your mind and not listening to its anxious thoughts. It also gets you more in tune with your body, and you'll notice both good and bad sensations faster. Follow the below steps to try out a body scan.

1. Get comfortable. It's usually recommended that you lay down, but if you're more comfortable sitting, do that (especially if laying down means you're going to fall asleep).

2. Close your eyes, or just lower them and let them become unfocused.

3. Decide where on your body you would like to start the scan. You can pick any spot you like, or decide on a systematic scan from your head to your feet. It's completely up to you how you want to do it. Once you're ready, intentionally breathe in and focus your attention on your body part of choice.

4. Focus on the sensations you feel in that area of your body. There could be tingling, pressure, buzzing, tightness, or temperature, or nothing at all. Keep your attention on that without any additional thought. Notice what's in the present

without any judgement.

5. Purposefully release your attention, then move to the next part of your body, and continue to focus on the feelings until you've moved across your entire being.

6. At the end of your scan, concentrate on expanding your attention to feel your whole body breathing.

7. Open your eyes, and mindfully move into the present moment.

At some point in your body scan, you'll realize that your mind has started wandering. That's completely normal, and it will happen less as you practice. Every time it happens, acknowledge that it is, then very gently guide your mind back to the sensations in your body. Don't be too forceful.

The body scan is one of the most beginner friendly forms of meditation, but you can find hundreds of different types. Experiment and choose the ones that suit you best. The goal is to be open, curious, and non-judgmental, and to simply experience what you feel in the moment. There are apps and websites that offer guided meditations as well. These are usually a person speaking softly and telling you what to concentrate on. Some might have relaxing music or quiet sounds in the background.

Mindfulness doesn't only apply to meditation. It's also a way to pay attention to what is going on in your daily life, and slowing down to notice the things you normally rush. The same principles apply, but instead of focusing on your breath and body, you're noticing the world around you. It's an antidote to the rumination that keeps the anxiety churning through your mind. Besides focusing on breathing, here are some more easy ways to pull yourself out of your head and into the moment.

- **Use your vision** – Notice the colors, shapes, sizes, types of movement, and whatever else you can observe about the things around you. Pick one of these aspects, like the color red, and find everything that fits it you can without changing your position. Repeat until you feel calmer.

- **Use your hearing** – What sounds do you hear right this moment? Even if you thought there was silence, when you tune in closely, you'll hear a little something. It may be the white noise of your computer fan you've long since tuned out, or the sound of your cat kneading at your bedspread.

- **Use your sense of touch** – Feel some of the textures of things around you. Feel the smooth top of your desk, or your dog's soft fur, or the roughness of a rock.

- **Use your sense of smell** – Light some of your favorite scented candles. Buy some essential oils that you enjoy. Walk outside and smell the fresh grass or the coming storm.

- **Use your sense of taste** – Give yourself a treat, like a square of chocolate, and focus deeply on how it tastes. See if you can pick out different flavor notes. Have a cup of tea or coffee and sip it slowly.

- **Take a walk** – Walk at the speed that's comfortable for you, wherever you feel like doing it. Notice the movement of your body and the muscles you use to walk. Pay close attention to your surroundings.

Once again, your journal is a valuable tool. Create mindful entries and write about your immediate surroundings. You can also try out automatic writing. Set a time for yourself, and write non-stop until it goes off. This is hard to do at first. If you get stuck, just write "I can't think of anything," or something similar. The important thing is that you don't stop writing. As you practice and get better at getting your thoughts onto paper, this is a great exercise for figuring out what exactly is on your mind. Practice it regularly.

Practice mindfulness whenever you have the opportunity. You can get started from the moment you wake up with mindful waking. As soon as you wake up, before grabbing your phone or doing anything else, sit in your bed or a chair and get comfortable. Relax but keep your spine straight, and close your eyes.

Notice the sensations in your body, and the renewal that it got from sleep. Take three deep breaths – in through your nose, out through your mouth. After releasing the third one, let your breathing go to its natural rhythm and focus on it. Notice the air entering and leaving your body, and the rise and fall of your chest and belly. As you do this, set an intention for yourself.

An intention is simply a statement of how you want to be during your day. Setting an intention gives your brain a more structured way to work, connecting the unconscious impulses with the conscious abilities in a productive way. It puts your unconscious mind to work throughout the day, as it will work towards your intention without you really noticing.

Your intention can be anything, such as "Today I will be kind and patient with myself and others," or "I will keep my motivation high today and get things done." If nothing immediately pops into your head, consider these questions for a starting point. Consider what people and situations you will face.

- What could I do today to have the best impact?

- What mental quality would I like to strengthen and grow?

- What do I need in order to take care of myself?

- How can I be more compassionate to myself and others during difficult times?

- What can I do to feel more connected and fulfilled?

Once you've set your intention, bring your

awareness back to the present and start your day. As you go, check in with yourself occasionally. Pause to take a few deep breaths and check in on your intention. What are you doing to work towards it, both consciously and subconsciously? The more you practice this, the easier it will become to meet your goals, and you'll find yourself happier and more productive throughout your day.

Eating is another opportunity to be mindful. It's pretty easy for us to pay very little attention to what we eat, only focusing on getting the meal done and getting on with the day. Oftentimes we'll finish something without even realizing, and be surprised that there's none left. Eating can be a wonderful experience, though. Eating mindfully takes advantage of this fact, and lets you satisfy not only your physical hunger, but some of your subtler senses and desires.

Breathe before you eat. Typically, we move from one thing to the next without pausing to consider what we're doing. Taking a moment to breathe gives you a calmer transition to your meals, and prepares you to eat mindfully. Close your eyes and focus your attention inwards for eight to ten breaths. Listen to your body, and see what your level of hunger is.

Don't think about the last time you ate, or what you had. What physical sensations tell you that you're hungry? Consider an emptiness in your stomach, a lack of desire to eat, shakiness, stomach growling, and other symptoms of hunger or a lack thereof. See what your body is doing with each of these things. How hungry are you at this moment?

Learn to eat based on your hunger. Eating for enjoyment or out of boredom are common practices, but eating when you aren't hungry is hard on your body. Use the feelings in your body to determine when, what, and how much you should eat. Your body gives you these signals for a reason, and listening to them will help you eat sensibly while still enjoying your meals.

As you eat, slow down and experience every bite. Really savor it, paying attention to all the flavors, textures, and scents. Enjoy what you're eating. If you aren't getting joy from something that you're eating, don't eat it. Only eat the things that you love, with a mind towards health, of course. Eating more slowly and noticing each bite not only gives you more enjoyment, it also gives your stomach more time to signal to you how much it needs. Eating too quickly doesn't give it that time, and you might end up overeating.

If you're getting regular exercise or physical activity, you can make improve your workout with mindfulness as well. Before you begin, consider what you want your aim to be. Decide what you want to be mindful of, and set that in your head. For example, before going out for a run, you could say, "I am going to notice the muscles moving in my legs, and concentrate on my breathing."

Warm up with simple moves for about five minutes. Focus on matching your breathing to the rhythm of your movement. This will get your brain activity, heart rate, and nervous system in sync with each other. Start your exercise, and keep your rhythm going. Even as you increase in intensity, keep everything synchronized. If it's difficult to do, start out by just focusing on your breathing, and it will get easier.

For the last ten to fifteen minutes of your activity, push yourself. Notice how energized you feel when you're challenging yourself. Cool down over the course of five minutes, gradually working into being still. Take in your surroundings. Finally, rest for five minutes. Feel the sensations in your body, and try to name them. Notice how much more awake and refreshed you feel.

Practicing daily gratitude is another great way to be mindful of the positive things in your life. Every day, write down three to five things that you're grateful for. These can be absolutely anything, big or small. You can do this in a morning for a cheerful start to your day, or before bed as a way to cap everything off.

Change your items each day so that none of them become something you mindlessly write down without thinking. As you write them, pay close attention to them – hold a picture of them in your mind's eye, think about the impact they have on your life, and focus on the happiness they bring you. You can expand this into more of a journaling prompt by writing these things next to the items. Or, keep it short and sweet, and simply list what they are.

There are no hard and fast rules when it comes to mindfulness. You can practice it through meditation, focusing on your breathing, taking in your surroundings, or getting your thoughts onto paper, or any other way you can think of. The main goal is to notice the positive things in your life and get out of your own head for a while. It grounds you in the present, not allowing you to dwell on the past or future. Be intentional in your mindfulness, and even when your mind starts to wander, gently guide it back and remind yourself of how much better you'll feel afterwards.

Chapter 7: Recognizing and Controlling Panic Attacks

"You don't have to control your thoughts. You just have to stop letting them control you." –
Dan Millman

Arguably one of the worst parts of anxiety disorders are panic attacks. A panic attack is the sudden and usually unexpected onset of deep fear or discomfort. It has a slew of symptoms it brings along with it, and everything peaks within just a few minutes. Typically, an attack will include at least four of the following:

- Increased heart rate, pounding heart, or palpitations

- Sweating

- Trembling/shaking

- Shortness of breath or a sense of suffocation

- Choking sensations

- Chest pain or discomfort

- Nausea or other stomach upsets

- Dizziness, light-headedness, or feeling faint

- Chills or hot flashes

- Numbness or tingling

- Feelings of unreality (derealization) or of being detached from yourself (depersonalization)

- Fear of losing control or "going crazy"

- Fear of dying

You'll recognize that these are mostly anxiety symptoms discussed near the beginning of the book. However, the difference is the intensity. Panic attack typically peak around ten minutes or less, then begin to fade. The symptoms are so intense many people end up in the hospital, believing they're suffering from a heart attack, breathing problem, or other serious illness the attacks can mimic.

These attacks occur suddenly, and can show up even when you're in an overall calm state. The trigger may or may not be obvious. Someone with social anxiety might have a panic attack just before giving a public speech. Attacks can be triggered in people with obsessive compulsive disorder if they are not able to complete their rituals. Pondering about a future event might cause an attack in someone with more generalized anxiety. Oftentimes though, there isn't an obvious cause. Practicing CBT should help you be able to identify the causes and work to avoid further panic attacks.

Panic attacks are so frightening and unsettling that the victim will fear having another one. Of course, this contributes to the overall anxiety, and therefore the potential for panic attacks. This fear isn't one that can be reasoned away, however, and that realization may cause even more anxiety. You can reduce your overall anxiety through CBT, and in this chapter, we'll discuss ways to control and avoid panic attacks. With those tools in your belt, your anxiety will be reduced to nothing.

If you've experienced a panic attack before, you already know what one feels like. The first couple may be completely terrifying and mysterious, but once you can identify them, you at least have the peace of mind that you'll be okay soon afterwards. That doesn't help in the moment though. If you're unfamiliar with panic attacks or didn't already know this, there are some signs leading up to the full-blown attack. If you're able to catch the symptoms early, it will be easier to put to a stop with the exercises listed further on.

An intense onset of any of the above symptoms indicates a panic attack. Some of them may show up before the actual attack, however. You might feel a sudden and deep fear that gradually starts to grow. A pounding heart and shortness of breath begin as soon as the amygdala has decided it located a threat. You could begin sweating, or feel as though the room is spinning.

With any luck, you may be able to recognize these symptoms for what they are before you're hit too hard. If you do, these coping mechanisms will be easier to accomplish and have a greater effect. If you're already in the midst of an attack, these will still help you and get you to come down faster. Decide which of these methods are best for you, and as soon as you recognize a panic attack, get started.

- **Deep breathing** – Focus on taking slow, deep breaths. Think of it as cancelling out the quick and shallow breaths that your anxiety is encouraging. Breathe in and out of your mouth, and focus on the air filling your chest and belly before slowly releasing it. Breathe in for a count of four, hold for one second, then exhale for a count of four.

- **Acknowledge the panic attack** – Just like you do with your negative thoughts in CBT, acknowledge that you're having an attack and name it. Tell yourself that your fear isn't real and will pass soon, and then you'll be alright.

- **Remove stimuli** – If you think your panic attack was brought on by too much happening around you, remove what stimuli you can. Close your eyes so that you don't see as much going on. If you're in a busy place and you're able, remove yourself to somewhere quieter.

- **Use mindfulness to ground yourself** – Go through all of your senses to ground yourself to your surroundings and get out of the panic in your mind. List five things you can see, five sensations that you feel, five things you can smell, five things you can hear, and if you have something you can use, five things you can taste. As you work your way through the list you'll gradually come down from your attack.

- **Pick a focus object** – This is another way to ground yourself. Find an object to focus on. Concentrate on it completely, and list every observation that you can about it. Use all of your sense that you can.

- **Relax your muscles** – Panic tightens up your whole body. Use a muscle relaxation technique to loosen its grip and get you to relax. Focus on relaxing one muscle at a time. Start small, with something like your fingers. Move your way throughout your whole body. This method is easier if you've practiced it before.

- **Find your happy place** – Think of a place that would be incredibly relaxing for you, like a cabin in the woods or a hammock on a beach. Picture yourself there, and fill in as many details as you can. Find something for all of your senses to engage with. Keep the scene calm and quiet.

- **Use a mantra** – Focus all of your energy on repeating a mantra in your mind. It can be something as simple as "This too shall pass," or one that has more personal meaning to you. It's helpful to come up with one while you're calm and have it ready to go as your lifeboat.

The main goal with any of these methods is to get out of your own head. The panic attack is caused by spiraling thoughts that build on each other and get worse and worse. You might not even be able to pinpoint what the thoughts are in the midst of your panic, but something is at the center of them. Getting your attention away from the thoughts and onto an outside source will take away their power. Getting your physical body under control forces it to calm down and return to normal, as well.

If you're unable to stop a panic attack before it hits, it will usually subside quickly but leave you feeling unwell afterwards. It's important to take care of yourself during this time as well. You just experienced a medical emergency, and while you may not have needed to see a doctor right then, it still took a lot out of your body. Even coming down from flight-or-fight mode during more normal experiences leaves you drained.

Be kind to yourself and do something you enjoy. Don't punish yourself or beat yourself up for having a panic attack. No matter what stage you are at in your treatment, it's not your fault. Remember that it's just a biological function that you're working on improving. You can look at it as similar to an allergic reaction. You can work to avoid both, but even with precautions they can't always be avoided. You wouldn't scold yourself for having an unintentional allergic reaction, so don't do it for an unintentional panic attack.

Once you've acknowledged the panic attack for what it is, do something relaxing or enjoyable. Write, draw, read, take a walk, get some gentle exercise, take a nap, play video games – whatever normally gets you into a peaceful state of mind. You're giving your brain a break while it recovers from the flood of cortisol it had. Don't engage in anything too taxing for at least a couple of hours, and maybe longer if you can. Think of it as both a break, and a way to get your mind off of the incident.

Relaxation techniques or meditation are great ways to come down from a panic attack as well. Practice your mindfulness techniques, perform a body scan, or use a guided meditation. You can relax your muscles by adding to the body scan – as you scan each muscle group, gently tense it for a few seconds, and then relax it. This way you will consciously relax each muscle, and find both your body and mind calmer afterwards.

You might even experience after effects of a panic attack over the next day or two. There could be sore muscles from clenching them too tightly, a leftover headache, some residual worry, or something similar. Do whatever you need to treat these as well. Just because a day has passed, it does not mean the panic attack never happened. Pay close attention to your body and mind and treat it as you need to, for as long as necessary.

Chapter 8: Gaining Self-Confidence

"Nothing can bring you peace but yourself."
– Ralph Waldo Emerson

Low self-esteem typically comes with anxiety disorders, and contributes to them. You might feel you're not as good as other people, or not worthy of anything positive that could come your way. The lack of confidence makes you fearful to enter new situations or engage with people, worsening anxiety and social phobias. CBT will help you with the anxiety, but it will also do you a lot of good to build up your self-confidence.

The way we talk to ourselves contributes significantly to how we see ourselves. Cognitive distortions will bring out the critic in your head, leading you to think things like "I'm not good enough," or "I'll never get this right." To get better, you need to change your self-talk. Evaluate it carefully, looking back through your journal if you need to.

Look at how you refer to yourself and what descriptive words you use. Now consider – would you say those things to a friend of yours? If a close friend made the exact same mistake as you when you called yourself stupid, would you call them the same name? Most likely not.

It's a difficult concept sometimes, but you get to be your own best friend. If you catch yourself thinking something negative about yourself, cheer yourself up just as you would a friend. Remind yourself of all the good in you, and how much progress you've made towards getting better.

Positive affirmations are a great way to improve your self-talk. These are phrases you can keep handy to talk yourself up when necessary. Get started by writing down all of your positive qualities. Be honest, and don't worry if you sound like you're bragging sometimes. Write everything, whether it's something general like your intelligence, or the specific way you handled a certain scenario.

Out of each quality you listed, come up with a simple phrase that you can have ready to go when you need it. It's easy to be hard on ourselves, but we need to remember our good qualities and use them to boost ourselves up.

There is something to be careful of when coming up with your affirmations. Don't get too outrageous, or your brain won't believe them. It will reject them and cling on tighter to the distortion it has, convinced that you've given it proof of its truth. Having an affirmation like "I am deliriously happy every day and my life is perfect," is clearly untrue. Be more subtle, and focus on the progress you're currently making. "I am improving every day" is a much better affirmation, and it's true.

Besides being your own champion, there are things that you can do every day to gradually build up your confidence. As your anxiety improves, you'll find it easier to do more of everything. When you feel able to put yourself out there for new experiences, being more self-confident will in turn reduce your anxiety further. Read on for some easy ways to get started.

Practice Confident Body Language

A huge part of how humans communicate is body language. Typically, we unconsciously move based on our mental state. You can actually reverse this and use purposeful body language to influence your mind. A lot of socially anxious people have very telling body language – trying to take up as little space as possible, avoiding eye contact, speaking quickly and quietly, moving in ways that help them hide from the gaze of others.

You're going to purposefully adjust your body language to broadcast confidence. Not only does this come across to other people, it will also signal to your mind to behave in a way that matches your movements and posture. Confident movements actually lower cortisol in your body and increase good hormones like serotonin and dopamine.

To signal confidence, work on your posture for both sitting and standing. Keep your back straight and your shoulders back. Your chin should be parallel to the ground. If you've had poor posture, correcting it will be uncomfortable at first. Keep it up though, and it will soon feel natural. You'll probably have less aches and pains in your shoulder, neck, and back, and less headaches if you suffer from them.

Learning to remain still is a huge step in showing more confidence. Anxious people are always tense, and it comes through in the body language. They feel they need to move often, and have jerky movements from the muscle tension. Start to notice these little movements you make. Simply being mindful of them can help you reduce them.

When you're standing, balance your weight between both of your legs and keep your feet about shoulder width apart. Refrain from tapping your toes or shuffling your feet. When sitting, keep yourself comfortably back in the chair rather than perched on the edge as if ready to jump up at any second. Keep your legs either apart or loosely crossed, however you're comfortable, but don't tap your feet or keep your legs tightly wrapped together.

Practice keeping your head still as well. Anxiety makes us actively seek out threats, but confident people can keep their gaze on a fixed point without worry. Fidgeting is another huge sign of anxiety. This might take a lot of work at first, but keeping your hands and fingers still will go a long way towards making you look and feel more confident.

Reduce the speed of your movements and speech. Anxiety quickens these things and it comes across to others. Walk at a slower pace with good-sized strides. Be mindful of your speech and choose your words before using them, then be sure to use a good speed rather than rushing. Add more pauses in your actions, rather than jumping from one thing to the next. Silence can also be your friend – it's okay to not be talking at every moment or breaking the quiet in some way, a thing anxious people often do.

Confident people have more open body language, while anxious ones are more closed off. Broadcast openness by exposing more of your body in subtle ways. Don't cross your arms or legs tightly. Lean back while sitting instead of scrunching forward. Imagine the difference in how you hold yourself in bitter cold and sweltering heat. Anxious body language fits well in cold weather, keeping limbs close and not moving too broadly to hold onto some warmth. Gradually move your body language into warmer territory – everything is more open and you keep your limbs farther away from your body.

Finally, work on being more direct in your body language. Maintain eye contact with people that you're interacting with. Smile often. Face the person you're communicating with and avoid looking around your environment. Think of the person you're with as a friend and ally, and let your movements towards them be open and friendly.

Break Out of Your Comfort Zone

Take some time to list the things you fear most. Organize the list and rank the items from least to most anxiety inducing. Once you've done that, start facing the fears. Start on the easiest item for you to accomplish, and work your way up to the most difficult. When you start, you might feel like you'll never have the courage to confront your biggest fears. As you gradually work towards them, however, you'll find that you can do it.

Your fears can be absolutely anything, from calling to make a doctor's appointment to skydiving and anywhere in between. Don't take into consideration how other people might feel about the things that scare you. These are your own fears, and even if anxiety has created some that feel silly, they're very real to you.

No Mistakes, Only Learning Opportunities

A big component of anxiety is being afraid to make mistakes. That can hold us back significantly, keeping us from trying new things or taking calculated risks. Change the way that you look at mistakes. They are never failures – instead, they are learning opportunities. No matter what mistake you've made or what the outcome was, you can find something to learn from it. Because of this, you can view mistakes in a more positive light. Everyone makes mistakes, but not everyone learns from them. By seeing them as valuable lessons, you've changed mistakes into something positive.

Laugh at Yourself

A lot of people filter their humor, but socially anxious people even more so. Work on loosening up a bit. Having a sense of humor goes a long way towards making every day more positive, and making it easier to brush off mistakes and bad experiences. You might have noticed that a lot of confident people are also funny, and vice versa. They're not afraid to make jokes at their own expense and laugh at them.

This can be hard at first, especially if you've spent years beating yourself up and only noticing the bad things you've done. It can help to imagine that you're in a really cheesy sitcom – when you experience something less than desirable, think of how it would be portrayed for laughs in that sitcom. You'll soon find how fun and ridiculous all of life can actually be.

Socialize

This is, of course, the big one for socially anxious people. You'll definitely need to work through your CBT before diving into new social situations. As you're able to calm your anxiety and find yourself less distressed at the thought of interacting with others, you can start to branch out and try new things. Just like any other skill you might learn, being social takes time and practice to be good at. So you need to do exactly that – practice.

Find some ways to get out more, like social events, hobby groups, or clubs. Choose ones that really speak to your interests, so that you feel comfortable in that regard. Start going to some of these, but as tempting as it might be, don't bring a friend. Going with a friend allows you to lean on them for support, or let them carry conversations and other interactions. It's much the same as trying to learn how to ride a bike but never taking off the training wheel. If you're feeling particularly anxious, you can bring a friend to some things at first, but your goal is to go alone and meet new people.

Don't go into social interactions with a goal for their outcome. Simply be with the other people. Make small talk or chat about your hobbies, but don't hold any expectations for what may come after. If you enter every social situation with the set goal of making a friend, finding a date, or getting approval from someone, you're only placing more stress on the situation than there needs to be, and you'll be disappointed if you don't get the desired result. Instead, view every interaction as practice, and congratulate yourself for doing it. If something more comes from the conversation, great, that's an added bonus.

When you get home from a new social situation, take some time to reflect on it. Get out your journal and write about it. At the very least, write down what the event was, when you attended it, and a couple of reactions or emotions you experienced. Keep this up for a while. You don't need to record every single social outing, but try to do so with ones that you had a somewhat strong reaction to. As you improve, you can look back at the older events and see how much your thoughts on the situations have changed.

Once you've overcome some of your anxiety fears, try your hand at making your own plans. Invite your friends over for a board game night, or to go to dinner at your favorite restaurant. Ask a small group of people to go to a baseball game with you. Think of what activities and outings you enjoy, and then ask people to join you. It's intimidating at first.

Social anxiety probably stopped you from asking anyone for anything in the past. It could have come from a fear of rejection, or the sense that you'd be bothering people by doing so. However, those are false beliefs you're well on your way to overcoming. Plan your own social activities and invite whoever you'd like.

Here are some journaling prompts to answer that will help you build your self-esteem.

- List everything that you like about yourself, big and small.

- What are your strengths?

- What type of situations do you excel in?

- What good qualities do you think others notice about you?

- Think of some recent compliments that you've received.

- Make a list of things that make you happy, no matter how little.

- What gets you excited?

- What are some positive events in your life that still have an effect on you today?

- What makes you unique?

- In what ways do I give to others?

- What would my life look like if I had 100% self-confidence?

- If I had no limits, what would I do with my life?

Chapter 9: Staying on Track

"No longer forward nor behind I look in hope and fear; But grateful take the good I find, The best of now and here." – John G. Whittier

So, you've made it to the end of the book. You've put in the work, learned the skills, and beaten your social anxiety. Where do you go from here? Well, the work never really ends. Keeping a healthy mind is just like keeping a healthy body – you have to maintain it and continue exercising. With any sort of treatment, the goal is to avoid a relapse. A full-blown relapse would be going back to your old ways of thinking, and letting cognitive distortions and anxiety take hold again.

It's completely normal to have some brief lapses, especially when things aren't going well. Try to anticipate some situations that might do this to you. At this healthier state of mind, when do you feel at your lowest? Is there anything that still causes a flare of anxiety? Are there any fears you haven't conquered yet? What does a bad day look like to you, and how does it make you feel?

It's impossible to avoid all bad situations in your life, but you can be prepared for them. Knowing what they might be ahead of time will allow you to build up some armor. However, even if something does hit you particularly hard, you've learned the skills to deal with it in a healthy way.

Keep up the practice of CBT and mindfulness. You may not feel the need to continue your negative thought log, but it can be helpful to revisit it, especially if you notice a trend of negativity. Don't be afraid to go all the way back to step one if you feel like you need to. Remember that these are now tools you have in your arsenal, and you can use them however and whenever you need to.

Just because you're in a better place now doesn't mean you need to stop everything you've learned to do. Continue to ground yourself and notice your surroundings with mindfulness. Use it to pull yourself out of your head if you find yourself in a negative spiral. Meditate regularly, which has been scientifically proven to have benefits for anyone and everyone.

Read on about some tips, tricks, and practices to help you stay in a healthy state of mind. These are great ways to exercise your brain and continue to improve.

<u>Journaling</u>

You can continue tracking your progress and improving yourself through journaling. You can continue your negative thought log, practice regular automatic writing, keep records of your day, write your thoughts and feelings, or whatever else you feel like using your journal for. There are endless ways to benefit from it. Check Chapter 10 for some journaling prompts.

Schedule Pleasant Activities

Make sure you're not only scheduling activities you must do, but also ones that you want to do. Not many people think to actively do this, even though it's important to living your best life. In fact, it's easy for us to fall into thinking that we need to be working constantly, and any time off or breaks are "slacking."

As you know now, you need that time to rest and recharge, and it does wonders for body and mind. Constant work will make you burnout, and it's hard to come back from that. You're going to avoid that by marking pleasant activities on your schedule and sticking to it, just like you would with any appointment on your calendar. You should have at least something small scheduled for each day.

"Pleasant activities" will mean something different for everyone. It can be something small, like relaxing at home, reading a book, taking a nap, cooking, or playing some video games. It might be something that gets you out of the house – going to the movies, social outings, dinner with family, a walk in the park. Consider what makes you happy and relaxes you. It doesn't have to be grandiose or fit anyone else's idea of enjoyment. It's for you and you only. Let go and enjoy the activity with all of your being, and embrace the break you're getting from your day.

Not only does this give your brain some much needed downtime, it also acts as a reward. Even though humans are vastly complex creatures, we still have the basic desire for reward and aversion to punishment. Positive reinforcement will always be more effective than negative reinforcement. These fun things you plan for yourself are a reward to your brain.

You're telling it that it's done a great job, so it gets to produce some serotonin and dopamine for itself. Rewards in themselves produce these happy hormones, so you're getting pleasure from the activity itself and from your brain enjoying the reward.

Look for Inspiration

The world around you is full of inspiration. This isn't only for artistic or creative people – inspiration can come to any of us, and give us strength and motivation. One of the most popular forms of inspiration is to look at quotes from famous or knowledgeable people. You've probably seen quite a few home décor items that feature a positive quote of some sort. Surround yourself with ones that speak to you. Write them in your journal, or stick them on your work computer with sticky notes. Actively seek out new sayings and ways of looking at the world from people that you admire.

Take time to soak in other forms of inspiration, as well. Find out what speaks to you. It might be paintings, songs, movies, dance, drawings, or a million other things. Admire the ones that give you that spark of joy. Experiment, and see if participating in one of these endeavors might further inspire you. Perhaps not, and you can just stick to viewing them. Learn about the masters in the craft that you enjoy, and the journeys they've been through.

Reading is a fantastic source of inspiration as well. You could look to ones such as this that give guidance and self-help, or true stories of other people's struggles and triumphs. Perhaps you enjoy fiction, and reading a good murder mystery or epic fantasy gets your brain working. Books provide a healthy distraction from our own troubles, and let us see into someone else's mind.

Get Involved in Something Meaningful

This can mean different things for different people. If you're religious, it could be attending sermons or gatherings, spreading your beliefs to others, or contributing time or money to charitable activities your organization is involved in. Besides religion, you might donate money or volunteer for a cause you care about. You might consider getting involved in community outreach programs for others that suffer from mental health disorders. If there aren't any support groups in your area, you could start one, or even get one going online.

Doing something that feels larger than you adds a lot of positivity and fulfillment to your life. Helping others to live better in whatever way you can is guaranteed to make you happier. It's impossible to think of the good things you've done and not smile. It's a wonderful thing to be able to help others while you're helping yourself.

Keep Your Physical Health Up

You probably already know that regular exercise can battle mental disorders like anxiety. When you're in the throes of mental illness, however, getting some physical activity might be the last thing on your mind. As your mental state improves, gradually work some exercise into your life. Even easy things like taking a walk outside can boost your mood and overall health. Yoga is great for beginners as well, as it focuses on stretching and loosening up your muscles as well as focusing on your breathing without being too intense.

Exercise should be fun for you. The ultimate goal is to get your heart rate up and challenge your body, not to injure it or overexert it. Pick an activity that meets these goals, and that you enjoy doing. There are an infinite number of things you can do, including ones that you may not have considered, like gardening or short walks around your house. Look into classes around you, if you think you'd have more fun in a group setting.

Exercise isn't the only aspect of your physical health. One thing that's easy to adjust is your diet. It can be challenging and take a lot of willpower, but the improvements in your health will be worth it. Anxiety can actually cause cravings for sugar, fats, and carbohydrates, as they fuel your body and your flight-or-fight response. However, too much of any of these can be bad for you. Work on consciously reducing some of these foods, and replace the short-term energy you get from them with long-term energy from healthy sleep and exercise.

Anxiety disorders can wreak havoc on your sleep health. Insomnia is a common side effect, which leads to fatigue during the day. A lack of sleep contributes to anxiety, and other health issues. As your anxiety lessens, you'll see an improvement in the amount of sleep you get and the quality of it. There are also habits you can incorporate to make even more of an improvement.

Pick a bedtime that works for you and regularly keep it as much as you can. Make sure your bedroom is as dark and quiet as you can get it. Even cover up your alarm clock with a cloth if it emits light. Your bedroom should primarily be used for sleeping, and not much else. Try to stop using electronics at least half an hour before bed. Experiment with your bedroom temperature, pillows, blankets, light levels, times, and whatever else you need to until you have the perfect sleep environment for yourself.

If you're still finding it hard to fall or stay asleep, try meditation just before bed. You can also try counting backwards from 300. Just as with meditation, if your mind wanders, gently guide it back to the countdown. If you reach zero, start again. Repeat until you fall asleep, though it usually doesn't take many repeats. Consider checking in with your doctor as well, to check for underlying issues that might affect your sleep. They might recommend you try melatonin, a gentle and non-addictive sleep aid you take before bed. There are also stronger prescription medications if necessary.

Work to keep yourself healthy. Ideally, you should have a primary care doctor that you visit often for checkups. They can give you guidance on diet and exercise, as well as catch any conditions that could be caused by or adding to your anxiety. If you're having difficulty working on your anxiety on your own, you can consider a medication to help you out.

Your doctor would be your first source of

information on something like that. Take steps to avoid illness and injury, and take any medication your doctor gives you as prescribed. Every system in our body depends on the others, so use the control you have to keep them as healthy as possible.

Reward Yourself

Give yourself a reward of some sort every time you reach one of your milestone goals. Do it when you accomplish something that's difficult for you. Do it when you overcome a new hurdle, or learn a new lesson.

We've already mentioned how effective positive reinforcement can be. When you've done something that you feel good about, rewarding yourself will make your brain want to do it again. Rewards don't need to be complex. It might be some extra time on one of your pleasant activities, or some food that you find indulgent. As long as you don't go overboard or reward yourself with something harmful to you, your options are endless.

Forgive Yourself

This fits in quite well with your new positive state of mind, and reframing mistakes as lessons. If you mess up somehow, forgive yourself immediately. A lot of anxiety comes from holding on to past mistakes and chewing them over in your mind constantly. However, you're past that now. Instead, you can simply acknowledge what happened, consider if you can learn any lessons from it, and move on.

Missteps will no longer ruin your entire day or plague you for weeks. Some people use the opposite of this idea as negative reinforcement – it may work a little, but it does more harm than good. Positive reinforcement and productive thoughts will always trump negativity.

Build a Support System

You may have some extra work to do for this, depending on the specifics of your social anxiety. If you have a couple close and supportive friends, you're already on your way. If you don't have many friends, or you aren't close enough to them or find them helpful to your mental health, the first thing you'll need to do is get out and meet some.

Again, get involved in more social activities, and don't worry about rushing anything. In the meantime, you can find a support group in your area or online. Even if you don't feel like you absolutely need something like that right now, connecting with people that have gone through similar struggles to you is immensely helpful. Being forced to work through your problems on your own only makes them more challenging.

If you have close friends and family that you can consider part of your support system, take some time to speak with them about what exactly you've been going through. Give yourself some prep time beforehand, and think of ways that you can speak to them about it. Anxiety can be difficult to speak about, and social phobias make it even harder. However, those that care about you will want to know what you're working through, and they'll want to help out in any way that they can.

Ask for exactly what you need. Most people aren't sure how to react to the suffering of others, and the default is to not show any reaction instead – human nature says that nothing is better than the wrong thing. However, if someone is told exactly what they can do to help, most will jump right on it. Decide what you need and want from your support system. It may differ from person to person, depending on your relationship with them.

Tell people if you just want to vent about something but aren't actually looking for advice. Ask for advice when you do want it. Tell people if you want them to question your actions so that you can notice them, or if you'd rather them ignore it if you seem a bit off. If you find that you absolutely need time out of your house every so often, tell the people you know so they can make plans with you. Reach out when you need more tangible help as well, instead of leaving yourself stuck with something and bringing on further anxiety.

Be prepared for the fact that some people may say they can't help you. It can feel completely crushing in the moment, but it's important to remember they're just as human and vulnerable as you are. Not everyone will be able to do everything that's asked of them. Your support systems needs to flow both ways – you can ask for help, but you also need to help them, and don't put undue pressure on them just for your benefit. Don't rely on others as your makeshift therapist, as well. Oftentimes that's too much burden on someone that's not trained for that sort of thing.

On the other side of the coin, don't let anyone into your support system that isn't actually supportive. Almost all of us know a friend or family member that actually does more harm than good in our lives. Regardless of how you feel, you are not stuck with these people. Being around someone that's unkind, dismissive of your problems, overly negative, and/or manipulative can cause you to slide back in your treatment. The people we surround ourselves with have a huge impact on us. It's okay to remove these people from your life, or at the very least severely limit your interactions with them. They cannot be considered as part of your support system.

Learn to Deal with Outside Negativity

You've learned how to deal with the negativity that your own brain produces. However, there are a lot of outside forces that are beyond your control. It might be other people you come across, big world events, or a situation that you can't easily remove yourself from. It's impossible to avoid any of this completely. There are ways you can build up your defenses and have healthy barriers, though.

We all know at least a couple of overly negative people, be it coworkers, family members, someone you often cross paths with, or even some friends. Not all of them will be obviously negative – they might seem cheerful in nature but still complain about everything, or disguise insults in concerned sounding statements, or some other subtle form of negativity. Even if it's not blatant, it's still bad for your mental health. Your best bet is to avoid these people completely, but that's not always possible in the real world.

When you're forced to interact with someone pessimistic, keep in mind that they have some sort of unhappiness in their life that they aren't coping with very well. Bring compassion to the forefront of your mind. After all, you've been there, and you might not have been pleasant to deal with when you were at your worst. It's impossible to tell what exactly is behind their personality, but dealing with them will become easier if you assume they're hurt rather than malicious.

Remember, however, you can't solve other people's problems. Unless someone directly asks or implies that they want your help, giving advice or otherwise giving unsolicited help will cause a lot more harm than good. They may take it as you saying they need to "fix" themselves. Besides, this puts too much burden on yourself. You can be a supportive and kind person, but you can't be someone's complete support system. Trying to take that on will be awful for your own mental health. Simply offer a listening and non-judgmental ear, and don't go beyond that unless called to and you know that you can handle it.

On a broader scale, your mental health can be affected by world events. The news has constant coverage everywhere you look. At any moment, there could be hundreds of bad things going on in any area, and there's a news source that's reporting on it. It's difficult to stop that from bringing you down sometimes. Whether it's something that's happening next door or around the world, compassion for other human beings will cause negative feelings when something is happening to them.

It's perfectly fine to disconnect yourself from the twenty-four-hour news cycle. Oftentimes we feel the need to be constantly informed, and that we shouldn't bury our heads in the sand. Some awareness of current events is important to have, but the news actually makes things seem a lot worse than they really are. Crime and violence have actually been trending downward in most parts of the world for the last few decades.

At the same time, access to the news has increased, and they've gained new methods of getting the story right away and in great detail. Bad news is what sells best, so modern technology gives us constant in-depth coverage of all that's happening. You really don't need to keep up on every detail to be an informed person. Turn off the news every so often. If you find you have a hard time doing that, schedule a block of time every day in which you're not allowed to check up on any news sources.

In the end, we can't avoid every source of negativity in life. It's not something you can control, but you can control your response to it. Look for the silver lining in everything and stay optimistic. Cut out any negative sources that you reasonably can, and build up your mental strength to handle the ones you can't. Acknowledge that you'll occasionally have some bad emotions, but don't let them take over your mind. CBT and mindfulness will be your best friends.

If you are comfortable talking about your struggles with mental health, consider supporting others in their own recovery. As mentioned in the previous chapter, you can find a local support group or start your own, in person or online. As you continue to grow and heal, you can help others do the same. This does a couple of things for you – it reinforces the lessons you've learned, and brings you personal fulfillment. Not to mention, you'll be helping someone else get to the point that you have, and improving their life. It gives you some extra motivation to keep going, as well. You'll have the desire to continue so you can be healthy and optimistic for those that you are mentoring.

Chapter 10: Q&A and Final Thoughts 1500

Congratulations on making it all the way to the end of *Social Anxiety*! You now possess the skills and strengths to overcome anxiety. Here we'll have some answers to frequently asked questions about the topics covered in this book, as a sort of quick reference guide you can refer back to.

- **Do I have an anxiety disorder?**

  o Occasional anxiety is a normal part of life. However, if you experience intense symptoms that continue for more than six months, you may have an anxiety disorder.

- **What causes anxiety?**

  o There's no one definitive cause for anxiety, and most people probably have it as a result of several factors.

Some known risk factors are having immediate family members with anxiety, suffering from prolonged or profound stress, trauma, certain health problems, specific personality types, and brain chemistry.

- **How are anxiety disorders treated?**

  o There are several treatment options, and their effectiveness can differ between individuals. Often time, the most effective method is some combination of these. Treatments include psychotherapy, cognitive behavioral therapy, stress management techniques, antidepressants, anti-anxiety medications, and beta-blockers.

- **What is obsessive-compulsive disorder?**

  o OCD is a severe form of anxiety that

160

is marked by repetitive thoughts and the need to engage in rituals. The repetitive thoughts are intrusive and often cause a lot of distress. The rituals, or compulsions, are a coping mechanism for the anxiety. They can be things like repeatedly checking to make sure the oven is off, checking that the door is locked several times an hour, or constant hand-washing.

- **What is social phobia?**

  o Social phobia, also known as social anxiety, is a fear of common social situations. It might be limited to one type of interaction, like public speaking, or in every potential social circumstance.

- **Is social phobia serious?**

  o Yes, though the severity differs

among people. It may prevent the sufferer from participating in very certain activities, or it may make them afraid to be in public at all. Victims may have a small group of friends, a few close friends, or no friends at all. It can have an impact on every aspect of life.

- **Is social anxiety common?**

  o Yes, it's actually believed to be one of the most prevalent psychological problems. A large number of sufferers report having symptoms for ten years or more before seeking treatment.

- **What's the difference between social anxiety and shyness?**

  o Social anxiety is characterized by an extreme fear of judgement or embarrassment. It's accompanied by physical symptoms like sweating, shaking, nausea, and blushing, among others. Shyness is simply the somewhat common fear of talking to new people or being in new situations, and can typically be controlled. Anxiety cannot be controlled without treatment, even when the victim is aware that their thoughts aren't realistic.

- **What is cognitive behavioral therapy?**

  o CBT is a proven form of psychotherapy that focuses on adjusting thoughts and behaviors to make them more positive. The basic steps are to recognize automatic thoughts (or cognitive distortions), challenge them, and replace them with positive thoughts.

- **How long does CBT take to work?**

  o This can vary by person, and the

163

amount of work they put into it. On average, professionals have reported their patients improving in 12 to 16 weeks.

- **What are automatic thoughts?**

  o These are statements or images that pop into your head throughout the day. Most people have some, but those suffering from mental illnesses are susceptible to their effects. Situations will trigger automatic thoughts that aren't based in reality, but that the sufferer then acts on, usually leading to something like anxiety or depression.

- **What is mindfulness?**

  o Mindfulness is intentionally noticing the current moment.

- **What are the benefits of practicing mindfulness?**

  o It develops the mind, increases awareness, improves focus, eases negative thoughts, reduces stress and anxiety, lessens depression, increases your sense of well-being, and improves sleep.

- **How do I meditate?**

  o Begin by simply focusing on your breathing. Take long, deep breaths, and notice each one. Work on moving your attention throughout your body.

- **How long do I need to meditate?**

  o You can see fast results from meditation in only ten minutes a day. Many people aim for about half hour sessions, but it's up to you and

165

the time you have available.

- **What is a panic attack?**

  o A panic attack is a sudden and intense onset of fear, along with other symptoms of anxiety. It can last between five and twenty minutes, and the sensations usually peak around ten minutes.

- **What are the symptoms of a panic attack?**

  o Possible symptoms include an extreme fear of impending death, sweating, pounding heart, accelerated pulse, fast and shallow breathing, chest pain, nausea, stomach pain, shaking, dizziness, and faintness, among others.

- **What do I do if I'm starting to panic?**

  o Find a way to ground yourself. Pick an object nearby or a physical sensation you can focus on, such as your breath. Concentrate on it and notice as much about it as you can. You want to get yourself out of your head, which is where the spiraling anxious thoughts are occurring.

- **How can I be more confident?**

  o Expose yourself to new experiences, conquer your fears, and be social. Practice the body language of confidence, to broadcast it to others as well as your own brain.

Journaling Prompts

For Stress Reduction

1. List ten things that make you happy.

2. Write about a recent problem in your life and how you handled it. Was it the best way? If not, how could you have done it

differently?

3. Think about a past mistake, and write only the positive lessons that you learned from it.

4. List everything you did well today, big and small.

5. Write about a positive difference you made in someone's life.

6. Who do you consider a positive influence, and why?

7. What problems are you currently facing that you have control over?

8. What problems are you currently facing that you don't have control over? What are some ways you can let them go?

For Setting Goals

1. What do you feel you're missing from your life?

2. What's the nicest thing you could do for

someone right now? How would that make you feel?

3. If you could open any business you wanted, risk free, what would it be?

4. If you had a financial planner, what would you ask them for help with?

5. What personality trait would you like to have, and how can you gain it?

6. What do you want to be doing in five years? Ten years?

7. How do you define success?

8. What are you most grateful for?

9. How would you like to be remembered in the future?

For Getting Thoughts onto Paper

1. What exactly are you feeling at this very moment? Include emotions and physical sensations.

2. Write the very first thing that comes to mind when you see the word "stress."

3. Write the very first thing that comes to mind when you see the word "pleasant."

4. What's something you're afraid of other people knowing about you?

5. If you could have anything you wanted right now, what would you ask for?

6. If you found a genie, what would your three wishes be?

7. What do you consider to be your guilty pleasures? Why are they "guilty?"

8. Take an online personality quiz. Write out your results, whether you agree with them or not, and why.

9. What's your mental happy place?

10. When do you feel the most relaxed?

11. When do you feel the most uncomfortable?

To Find Inspiration

1. What is your favorite song, and what do you like about it?

2. What was your dream as a child? Has it changed?

3. Do you have a favorite artist or art style?

4. How can you add more inspiration to your daily life?

5. What's a quote you find inspirational, and why?

Mindfulness

1. Write about your most recent meditation session, and how it made you feel.

2. Take your journal somewhere new, and write everything you're experiencing.

3. Write about yourself in the third person, as though you were an outside observing yourself.

4. What areas of your life could you slow down?

5. Write your mindful observations in the form of a narrative story.

Gratitude

1. What activities bring you the most joy?

2. What made you smile today?

3. Describe your favorite knick-knacks. The smaller, the better.

4. What are you looking forward to in the coming year?

5. What is the last thing that made you laugh?

6. What personal qualities do you like about yourself?

7. What qualities do you like in your close friends/family members?

8. Do you have a friend you can always depend on? Who are they, and why?

9. Write about your favorite memory with each of your family members.

10. What was the last movie or TV show you enjoyed, and why?

11. What is your favorite book? Why?

12. What cheers you up without fail?

13. What's your most favorite gift you've ever gotten? Why? Who gave it to you?

14. Think of a negative experience you've had, and list all the good things that came from it.

15. What charities do you support, or plan to support in the future? Why?

16. Describe a time that a stranger did something kind for you.

17. Describe a time that you did something kind for a stranger.

18. Set a timer for three minutes. Write about what you're thankful for until it runs out.

19. Write a detailed thank you note to your best friend.

20. Think of five people who you could send thank you cards to for small reasons.

Memory Improvement

1. What's your earliest memory? Be as detailed as you can.

2. If you wrote a memoir today, what would be in it?

3. Describe your best friend from grade school in as much detail as possible. Are you still friends with them? Why or why not?

4. Do you own objects that are tied to specific memories? Write about them and their associated memories.

5. Select a photograph from a pleasant memory and write the sensory details you experienced.

6. What new memories are you hoping to make in the next year?

For a Sketch/Art Journal

1. Draw your current emotions.

2. Fill an entire page with ballpoint pen doodles.

3. Open the dictionary to a random word. Create a collage based on it.

4. Practice gesture drawings in different colors and materials.

5. Pick a random page from your favorite book, and draw that scene.

6. Illustrate your favorite quote.

7. Create a portrait representative of you after reaching all of your goals.

8. Illustrate what you want your future to look like.

Conclusion

Thank you for making it through to the end of *Social Anxiety*, let's hope it was informative and able to provide you with all of the tools you need to achieve your goals whatever they may be.

The next step is to keep working on yourself, and refer back to this book whenever you need to. You should have learned some useful techniques for overcoming anxiety, social phobias, and panic attacks. You can continue the cognitive behavior exercises to gain even more benefits. Continue building up your self-esteem and trying new things. Lean on your support system when you need to, and keep it strong. As your phobias and anxiety decrease more and more, branch out and find new adventures.

If you know someone who is going through similar struggles to your own, share this book with them. If you're comfortable, talk to them about your experiences during your recovery and the things that helped you along the way. Helping others is a great form of therapy in and of itself.

Finally, if you found this book useful in any way, a review on Amazon is always appreciated!

Printed in Great Britain
by Amazon